TROUT & SALMON OF THE WORLD

TROUT & SALMON OF THE WORLD

SILVIO CALABI

THE WELLFLEET PRESS

Publishing Director: Frank Oppel
Editorial Director: Tony Meisel
Design Director: Carmela Pereira
Editor: Theresa Stiles
Composition: Meadowcomp Ltd.
Origination: Regent Publishing Services Limited
Printing: Leefung-Asco Printers Limited

Manufactured in Hong Kong
ISBN: 1-55521-665-X

Contents

Introduction

TROUT AND SALMON are predators that live in cold, clean water, fresh or salt. They eat mostly insects, crustaceans and each other. They have a small, fat fin on their backs just before the tail and are covered with a protective coating of slime. In body form, they tend toward the sleek and streamlined in a way that embodies speed, strength and grace, and to millions of us the salmonid shape expresses the very essence of "fish." Their colors are remarkable. The chrome plating of the fresh sea-run salmon proclaims it a special thing, as does the rosy blaze along the flanks of the rainbow trout and the multi-hued flanks and spots of the brook trout. On dry land, only birds and insects—the tropical variants, at that—rival the salmonids in the profusion and intensity of their tints. A surprising thing for the temperate and subarctic order of creatures whose neighbors, above and below the surface, run to sensible browns and blacks.

While their eyesight, their hearing and their sense of smell and taste are remarkably acute, their brains are not. Fishermen admire the selectivity of the wily trout or the stubborn salmon that refuse their baits, but this has much less to do with intelligence than it does with instinct. (In a heavily fished stream, it might be conditioning. Biologists say that cutthroat trout in the Buffalo Ford section of Yellowstone National Park have been caught—and released—on the average 17 times each. A conditioned response to an artificial fly comes rapidly, at that rate.)

Trout and salmon have become the stuff of dreams, legends and hard-won holidays. Literary traditions and lifestyles have been built around them. They were not always treated so reverently as now, however, although their estimable qualities as both gamefish and table fare have been praised on paper since long before Gutenberg began printing. In modern times—to the fisherman, modern

A landlocked salmon and an angler play out their duel on Nova Scotia's Shubenacadie River. When such a fish is released uninjured, everyone wins. Photograph by Gilbert van Ryckevorsel.

times reach well back into the 19th century—commerce and industry have rose and fell with the boom or bust of trout and salmon populations. Not merely in the "harvesting" of these fish for the table, but also in the manufacture and sale of fishing tackle. Only a few generations ago, whole watersheds were stripped of their trout so that they could be served in restaurants and sold in markets. Salmon were netted with no thought for the future. And loggers, miners, builders, farmers, papermill and power plant operators destroyed salmonid habitat all over the world. (They still do, if slightly less freely.)

That trout and salmon "eat well" is sometimes overlooked now, when the catch-and-release ethic has become so strong that relatively few rod-caught fish ever actually show up on a plate. Although sportsmen were releasing their catch for metaphysical reasons even in medieval times (a 14th-century epic poem called *Piers of Fulham* scolds anglers who don't throw little fish back to grow up—yes, the biology was backwards, but the sentiment was good), much historic admiration for trout and salmon likely sprang as much from the way they taste as from the way they look or take a hook. Today we no longer regard wild trout and salmon as prime food species (though a few still are), but interestingly enough the delicate way they sit upon the tongue is nevertheless directly related to their value—not as gamefish, but as environmental indicators.

Their diet colors and flavors their flesh, delicate white to deep red, and the temperature and velocity (if any) of the water they live in keeps it firm. Just as any organisms, trout and salmon are in a sense what they eat, and these noble fish eat well and live cleanly, or die. Their presence—their *natural* presence, not just the fact that a hatchery truck dumped them recently—in a body of water virtually guarantees their health. Naturally reproducing wild salmonids are the Good Housekeeping Seal of Approval on a stream or pond. Healthy populations mean the water is cool, oxygenated, and chemically balanced. Their presence means that aquatic insects, crayfish, freshwater snails and baitfish thrive there; and that the predator-prey equation is in proper equilibrium.

BUT FACTS are cold, dry things. Let the presence of these fish lift our spirits and comfort our minds. Salmon swimming in fleets upstream to dig their nests and lay their eggs represents a primal force of nature, just as surf coming ashore or geese crowding the ancient migratory flyways. To peer closely into the complicated hydraulics of a stream pool and finally make out the strong, undulant shape of a hunting trout is a true victory. As the third millennium of civilization begins, the men and women who wade the world's rivers and float her lakes in pursuit of trout and salmon are on a quest. They intend to re-insert themselves briefly into the natural order, so that they may return refreshed to their non-natural lives.

North America

THANKS MOSTLY to the intervention of state and provincial fish and game departments, it is no longer accurate to say that trout inhabit the northern half of North America and that salmon are found only along the Atlantic and Pacific coasts. Nor can we say that brook trout, native to northern New England and eastern Canada—or rainbow trout, which belong in watersheds that drain to the northwestern coast, or the cutthroat trout of the Rocky Mountains, or the lake trout of the deep, cold north-central waters—are still at home there. Or rather that they can be found there *only*, or in their pure form. All these species, and many more, have been transplanted all over the continent—all over the world, in fact—and have sometimes been cross-bred with each other, accidentally and intentionally. Today there are "eastern" brook trout from Alaska to Chile to Tasmania. California rainbows in Michigan and Vermont and (by way of Europe) South Africa. Pacific coho salmon swim out of Lake Ontario to to try to spawn in New York State rivers. And sea-run and landlocked Atlantic salmon have been shipped to virtually every coldwater state and foreign country ever since Maine began raising them as an export commodity in the 1870s.

A transplanted native becomes an exotic, and an exotic salmonid is a frustration to the ecological purist who treasures each distinct species, subspecies and strain of fish wild and pure within its own natural habitat. An exotic is a blessing, however, to millions of fishermen, who without them would have fewer trout, or maybe even no trout, to admire and pursue at home. Today, the best example of a worldwide exotic is the brown trout, favored by canny anglers everywhere as the top "trophy" trout, a stubborn and worthwhile catch. Brown trout are not native to North America at all. They are the native trout of Europe, originally dispersed from Spain to the Caucasus Mountains of Azer-

baijan and northward from Arctic Siberia to Iceland. In America they are still known to an older generation of sportsmen as "German" browns (a designation that slipped out of favor, for reasons that should be obvious, in the 1940s). And they were indeed German. The first shipment of brown trout eggs was sent to a hatchery in Long Island, New York, in 1883 by Baron Lucius von Behr.

BROWN TROUT

IN APRIL 1984, the centennial anniversary of the first successful planting of these von Behr browns was celebrated by a historically accurate re-enactment. Members of the Izaak Walton League ceremoniously deposited, from a milk can, 2,000 trout fry into the North Branch of Michigan's Pere Marquette River, near the town of Baldwin. On April 11 a century earlier, a certain J.F. Ellis and his assistant, using milk cans, had transferred almost 5,000 brown trout fry from a U.S. Fish Commission railcar into the cold, slightly tannic flow of the North Branch. Those fish were born from a second shipment of trout ova that von Behr had sent across the Atlantic; an earlier batch didn't survive the long ocean passage. American trout fishing, as has often been said, was changed forever.

Not all American browns are descended from these Teutonic trout, however; the others were part

(above) A fly-caught brown trout in the Rush River of west-central Wisconsin, photographed by Don Blegen.

(left) North America: A variety of trout and salmon unlike any other on earth. This cowboy fly fisherman in the Bridger Wilderness in Montana needs no hip boots. Photograph by Tony Oswald.

A classically marked small brown trout from Pennsylvania's Fishing Creek. Photograph by B&C Beck.

of a small but significant "species dispersal" that took place long after the earth's continents drifted apart and the Bering land bridge sank to part North America and Asia. It had nothing to do with climate or glaciation, either; it came about because of the tremendous political clout of the British Empire and the ethnocentrism of its servants. The British, inveterate globe-trotters who unhesitatingly felt their way of life was superior, did more to spread their sort of fishing (and shooting) sports than probably any other group of people. They were in the right places at the right times to do so, when the Industrial Age was spilling out of western Europe. In Victorian times and earlier, with a disregard for native species that today would stir the wrath of geographical societies everywhere, British military men and commercial travelers and fortune-seekers transplanted "their" trout and salmon (and gamebirds and red deer and so on) all over the earth in order to ease the burden of serving in the far-flung outposts of the Empire. While assuring ourselves that we would never be so ecologically insensitive, at least now, most of us are glad that *they* were, and continue to take advantage of their well-meant "mistakes." In actuality, the introduction of non-native species is now illegal in most countries.

But bringing fish and animals to North America would be like bringing sand to the beach; there was already an eye-popping variety and quantity there. Of the nine or so true trout on the North American continent today, only one came from Britain (Scotland, in fact)—the second of our brown trout. The descendants of those fish, which were brought to America in 1885, are still sometimes classified as Loch Leven browns.

As their name implies, the Loch Leven trout were a stillwater strain, silvery as salmon at certain seasons. Von Behr's stream-dwelling German fish bore the red and black spots and the saffron flanks that today identify a brown trout to us. The two subspecies have interbred, however, as all trout can, with varying degrees of ease, and today variations among North American browns are generally more due to environmental differences than to any original genetic traits.

America has always been a land where immigrants may prosper, and the brown trout did so with a will. And, as many an immigrant race, it was vilified and disparaged for some time after its arrival. Browns could tolerate a broader range of water conditions than brook trout. Brown trout are also superb predators, and in a stream where both fish live, the browns generally grow larger and more plentiful. Anglers weren't pleased to see their hometown-favorite fish squeezed out, or so it seemed, by the newcomer. But the brook trout was hit much harder by steadily worsening water quality—as pollution and habitat destruction spread in the early years of the 20th century—than it was by the rival brown trout. Small brook trout, much easier to catch than brown trout, fell victim to market "harvesting" too.

As time went by, fishermen began to appreciate the brown for its own qualities. It was surely a beautiful gamefish, though more subtly colored than the brookie; it did grow very large and strong; and it was undeniably more of an angling challenge than any native trout—brook, rainbow, laker, or cutthroat. In time it reached its present status, that of the premier American freshwater gamefish. Chances are that many anglers today have no idea that the species is *not* native.

Brown trout occasionally reach 30 pounds or more, under favorable conditions in clean, deep lakes, at the feet of large dams, or in stream pools where food is plentiful and competition and

This 18-inch fall brown trout of Montana's Madison River has nearly reached his full spawning colors. Photograph by Tim Leary.

predators are not. The perception in the United States today is that for big browns—3 to 5 or 6 pounds—the rivers of the West are best, while Eastern streams produce browns topping out at around a pound or two. That might have been so a couple of decades ago, but the sizes seem to be evening out a little more now, as angling pressure increases in the West and conservation and stream clean-up efforts (and, to be fair, certain hatchery programs in the Great Lakes region) pay off in the East.

In light of the general idea that trout are northern fish, it's interesting to see that the current American record brown trout, a 33-pounder, was caught in the White River in 1977; that's the White River in *Arkansas*—which has also given up two other line-class record browns. The all-tackle record—35 pounds, 5 ounces, was taken in southern Argentina in 1952. (The brown trout emi-

(far left) A small mid-summer brown trout, also from the Madison River.

This 21-inch brown trout of Montana's Big Hole River, caught on a Yuk Bug fly, has successfully made the switch to feeding on more than merely aquatic insects. Photograph by Tom Montgomery.

grated very successfully to other countries as well.) Every Patagonian fisherman worth his *vino tinto* will tell you of the 40-pound brown caught by a friend of his uncle . . . and it's probably true.

The consistently *biggest* wild brown trout on earth at the moment are probably the sea-trout of Tierra del Fuego, which commonly exceed 12 to 15 pounds. The *finest* brown-trout fishery on earth, in terms of a high-quality angling experience that often yields a beautifully marked 5- or 6-pound (or 8- or 10-pound . . .) fish each day, is probably New Zealand's. But for sheer numbers—pounds, population, and even fishermen—nothing beats the Salmon River and environs where it flows into Lake Ontario north of Syracuse, New York. Thousands of browns between 10 and 20 pounds swim out of the lake every fall and winter into the rivers to try to spawn. On shore and in the lake, thousands of fishermen wait for them, and for the huge fleets of chinook and coho salmon and steelhead (rainbow) trout that also arrive. At the height of the run, it can look like an angling circus, with bait, lures, flies, and snagging rigs so thick in the water that divers periodically go below to "harvest" the incredible amount of terminal tackle that is lost on the bottom.

Sea-run browns (the sea-trout beloved by European anglers) or migratory lake-dwelling brown trout often resemble Atlantic salmon, at least until the full spawning colors emerge. They are bright silver with black backs and black spots, and they often reach the size of salmon too. But distinguishing them is easy. Brown trout spots are truly spots—circular—while the salmon's markings are X-shaped. Trout usually have more spots as well, and at least some of them are surrounded by halos of lighter color. A sure way to identify the fish is by their vomerine teeth, in the center of the roof of the mouth. Brown trout have a well-developed double row of these teeth, but salmon only have one row, and some teeth may be missing. Fortunately, sea-trout and Atlantic salmon, despite their similarities, do not cross-breed in nature.

A brown trout in its fall spawning dress is a sight to behold: gold and green bodied, red and black spotted. Like salmon, larger males develop hooked jaws that, in combination with the well-fed brown's broad shoulders, humpback, and deep body, give them a highly aggressive appearance. This bullish look is borne out by the way they fight when hooked, often diving deep and slugging it out with massive head-shakings and dodging under snags and around river rocks. Like all trout, both stream- and lake-living browns feed primarily on aquatic insects, which makes them a prime quarry for the fly fisherman. But the larger fish learn to find protein in bigger chunks; they become cannibals, ambushing and eating smaller trout, leeches, snails, crustaceans, shiners and other baitfish, and even frogs, mice and the occasional hapless small bird. (That's how they got so big.) These fish are much more difficult to take on flies, and then the lure and bait fisherman enjoys the upper hand.

In friendly comparisons, when every judgment of strength and color and fighting ability has been made, brown-trout fans eventually play their ace—browns, especially those big ones, are caught far less often than big rainbows or brook trout or cutthroats. This is the challenge of the brown trout, the difference that makes it a truly superior gamefish. There is much truth to this, but brown trout are not necessarily cagier or more intelligent. However, they are very wary and, unlike their three popular cousins, generally nighttime feeders, while we are generally daytime anglers. The large trophy browns are often caught by those who prowl the streams at night and who learn to stalk, cast, strike and fight fish by feel rather than by sight.

BROOK TROUT

THE BROWN trout and the cutthroats are in the genus *Salmo*. Rainbow trout were recently reclassified from *Salmo* to *Oncorhynchus*, so were the Pacific salmon. And the brook trout, to confuse the picture a bit further, is actually a *Salvelinus*. Thus two of the four best-known North American "trout" are really a salmon and a charr. Confusion has reigned ever since Linnaeus himself misnamed his Swedish charr in 1758 (more on that later). Everyone agrees that charr are arctic salmonids, found in high latitudes all around the northern icecap, but there is no agreement on specifically which charr are species and which are subspecies. Biologists claim there are as many as a dozen recognizably different charrs, such as the brook trout, the lake trout, and the Dolly Varden, in the Americas alone.

This heavily spotted, chunky, well-fed brown trout from Wyoming's Bighorn River is living testament to the superb coldwater fisheries of the Rocky Mountain region. David Lambroughton photograph.

A brown trout that struck a Muddler Minnow streamer in Alberta's famous Bow River, near Calgary, and was photographed by R. John Sinal.

Autumn on Pennsylvania's lush Letort Spring Run: a wild brown trout lies in the net from which it is about to be released. Photograph by B&C Beck.

There is no confusion, however, about the brook trout, which, considering the east-west flow of colonization in North America, became our "first" trout, the one that figures so largely in the early history of American fly-fishing. Until the brown trout arrived in the 1880s, the brookie, or speckled trout, was to nearly all American fishing writers the *only* trout. (Although a few had traveled to the Rockies and were familiar with "mountain trout"—the cutthroat.) For the same reasons, the brookie was also the first trout to be nearly loved to death—overfished, almost wiped out—and the first to be "hatcheried" and subjected to endless experiments on breeding a fish with lower standards of living. The famous fish culturist Seth Green opened the first commercial American hatchery in 1864, in New York State, to raise brook trout for release into the wild to augment those diminishing populations. Ever since, as far as the real brookie goes, it's been downhill all the way. Records from

A small wild brown trout in the Mettowee River of southwestern Vermont. Photograph by Tim Leary.

the 19th century indicate that "squaretails" of 8 and 9 pounds were taken every year in the States; but today, even in the remote streams and lakes of northern Maine or Wisconsin, a 3-pounder makes the local newspapers. The big fish are found only much farther north, in what is still true wilderness. The International Game Fish Association all-tackle record is a 14-pound, 8-ounce brook trout caught in Ontario's Nipigon River in 1916.

That is not to say that today, in clean and remote mountain streams, lakes and beaver ponds from Labrador to Minnesota and down as far as the southern Appalachians, healthy populations of wild brook trout don't exist. They do, and perhaps in greater numbers than in the 1960s. Brook trout have also (barely) taken hold in the Rocky Mountain states and, in certain places, as far north on the West Coast as Alaska. But most of these non-native fisheries, healthy and wild and naturally re-

A stillwater brown trout taken in an un-named beaver pond somewhere in the high country of Yellowstone National Park. Photograph by David Lambroughton.

American classics: a Royal Coachman dry fly posed against the flank of a soon-to-spawn brook trout. Photograph by Don Blegen.

producing as they may be, are small. The true native, the product of a wild gene pool culled by predators and climate, is a vibrant, sharply detailed and brightly colored fish that cannot be reproduced in a tank. Of all salmonids, brook trout are perhaps the most difficult to relocate. They have very specific (and narrowly defined) needs in water temperature and chemistry and they do not seem to tolerate the presence of man. Yet in some respects they appear to be more tolerant than browns or rainbows; they can spawn successfully in lakes (which is why they were commonly used to replace the cutthroat trout that had vanished from so many high Rocky Mountain lakes) and they can stand greater alkalinity and acidity. For a century, brook trout (mostly Maine stock) have been laboriously transplanted all over the world, from Australia to Spain, but the only place they really took to is southern Patagonia, in the lakes and rivers of Chile and Argentina. Brook trout there reach sizes that rival their Canadian cousins.

Hatchery programs now do their best to help re-introduce brook trout into the native water they vanished from. One type of brook trout that has not been well re-established is the "salter" the sea-run fish of the New England coast. There are a few still, in little-known but prized Cape Cod streams, for example, but they've been supplanted by imported brown trout. The salter name is now slowly being transferred to the browns in those streams that have gone out to sea.

Delicate and jewel-like in small sizes, awesome and powerful as large fish, brook trout are spectacularly colored, the aquatic version of the male wood duck. Their lower fins are red-gold, edged in black and white, and in male fish, particularly in the fall at spawning time, this color extends up onto their bellies. Their green-black backs are handsomely decorated with wavy lighter markings, and scattered along their lateral lines are handfuls of red or purple dots within blue halos. In eastern Canada, brook trout and arctic charr often share the same water, and fishermen can see that the similarities between these two *Salvelinus* far outweigh any differences.

The 8- or 10-inch brookies of northern U.S. streams and ponds, the ones that generations of kids have dangled worms for, sometimes seem too dumb for their good, competing for the bait as sunfish do. Their problem is often overpopulation, too much competition for too little food. In severe cases, the fish may have skinny, underfed bodies and disproportionately large heads. However, even where the natural balance is proper, these fish rarely live longer than three or four years or exceed a pound. Big brook trout—true around the world, wherever these fish have been introduced—need big water, from God's River in Manitoba to the famous Minipi watershed of Labrador . . . .

LABRADOR REDS

LOG ENTRY, Minipi Camp, Labrador, summer 1981: *"Where are the 1 1/2-4-pounders!?"* The anonymous writer is referring to brook trout. It's no complaint, however, as the next entry explains: ". . . the group took and released 41 trout. Average weight 5 1/2 pounds. One 7 1/2 pounds, another 7 1/4 pounds." If you'd care to do the mental arithmetic, the group mentioned was made up of six anglers; the catch spanned a period of five and a half fishing days. And such totals are quite normal, even conservative, for the Minipi River. It may be the best brook-trout fishery in the world, if you measure best as *biggest*, and not *most*.

For river fishing, it's much like still water. The Minipi River, in the wild region southwest of the

Labrador reds: a stunning 5-pound native brook trout caught (and released) in the Atikonak River. Photograph by James Butler.

A tiny native brookie, the jewel of northern New England's mountain streams. Photograph by Tim Leary.

twin villages of Goose Bay and Happy Valley, is a lazy chain of lakes and ponds connected by short, shallow stretches of fast water. Jack Cooper, owner and operator of Minipi Camps (he and his wife, Lorraine, now have three lodges, several lakes apart), and his guides ferry their anglers around in motor canoes and skiffs. Most of the fishing is done from these boats. The oxygenated stream sections, where one can wade, are more productive when the lakes are low and warming.

To anglers accustomed to 10-inch brookies, these "Labrador reds" are simply shocking. Newcomers who see the mounted trout on a cabin wall often dismiss it out of hand as an exaggeration, but the size and the vibrant colors are true to life. A seven-pound brook trout reared in these cold but fertile waters is often only 24 inches long. The mass is packed in the broad, humped iridescent-black backs, and in the full stomachs, tinted that brilliant red-orange gold.

Vermont's famed Battenkill is the home of this 12-inch brook trout, photographed by Tim Leary.

Meager research indicates that these fish grow about 1 pound annually, and that some individuals may live 10 years or so. In recent times, many trout of 8 pounds or more have been caught there, and currently the Minipi holds five of the six International Game Fish Association world flyrod records for brook trout—fish that ranged in weight from 8 pounds, 4 ounces to 10 pounds, 7 ounces. All were caught in the 1980s. The all-tackle IGFA record, a 14-plus-pound brook trout, was caught in Ontario, but that was in 1916, when likely no sportfisherman had ever visited interior Labrador. Lee Wulff was the first to explore and then publicize Labrador's trout and salmon fishing, and that was only in the late 1940s and early '50s. Labrador fish are large, but populations are not. Cooper estimates that three years of unrestricted fishing would wipe out the trout in his leasehold. That record fish continue to be caught there speaks well for his stewardship of the resource.

Don Blegen caught, photographed, and released this vivid brook trout in western Wisconsin's Cady Creek.

Everything about this land is unusual. It resembles no other wilderness I've seen. From 1,500 feet in a helicopter, Labrador looks weathered and worn, ancient country furred with black spruce and balsam. On the low, glaciated hills, scabs of birch show pale green over burn scars. Water fills the irregular contours, and you have to wonder if a still-better trout river exists just over the next cluster of moraines—unknown, because no one has ever cast a lure or fly there.

Even very late in the 20th century, all civilization's glossy toys are barely enough to assure year-round comfort here. The trip to Goose was by Boeing 737, but the plane stopped in Wabush, Lab City and Churchill Falls first, like a rural bus making the rounds. When the whine of the jet spooled down, the severe flavor of the land began to penetrate the stillness. The 737, and the clusters of sophisticated helicopters and military aircraft moored around the airfield, belongs; this is a forward

Living treasure of the Mistassini River, Quebec—a 6-pound male brook trout, photographed by Tim Leary.

post holding at bay the Canadian North.

Jack Cooper's camps are log houses perched on points of shore that protrude into a large swelling of the Minipi generally known as Anne Marie Lake. The drill is simple. Each morning, after a back-woods breakfast that wards off the early chill and the line squalls that may sweep down the water-shed, we set off with our guide for the day. It was an hour's churn by outboard canoe, in that first week of July, to where the trout were feeding actively, in an arm of the main lake called Petch's Pond, after a fisherman who performed some notable deed there in the dim past.

The first hour of each morning was the same. Acres of water bordered by gloomy scrub forest, the stillness broken only by wind and by two fly lines whistling out from the canoe, continuously probing the points of the compass. When the first fish comes, it's startling. First there was a large

Early in the 20th century, northeastern "speckled trout" were successfully transplanted as far west as Alaska. This prime example of a stream brookie was caught in Oregon's Fall River. Photograph by Christine Fong.

dry fly bobbing on a mindless expanse of water with not a single natural insect for company. Then, with deliberation, a vast metallic form arcs from the water behind the fly and rams it down without a sound. There's time to note a full hand's-breadth of trout back—emerging here, disappearing there, with some of the same majesty of the great marine mammals. A sail-like fin, a strong, square tail, and that vigorous speckled curve. And then an irresistible force against rod and reel.

Fishing with a six-weight line and a five-pound-test leader tippet, I managed to net about half the fish I struck. Unlike brookies (the diminutive is highly inappropriate here) I've caught elsewhere, these seemed quite wary. Perhaps *selective* is the better term, because repeatedly during a hatch, trout rose within spitting distance of the canoe when a hooked fish was going through the final thrashing before being netted. Did those other fish regard this surface activity as a sign of heavy feeding?

The most enjoyable fishing was during the immense *Hexagenia* hatches. Hummingbird-size green and brown mayflies struggled from the water everywhere, when the surface temperature hit about 60 degrees, and especially when the sun had been out for a while. Daily, acres of fishing water became stippled with what must surely have been hundreds of pounds of biomass. And here and there we found one or two or several huge trout feeding very selectively.

Instead of vacuuming up whole lines of flies at a pass, these fish picked and swam, nibbling for all the world like spoiled children completely assured of their next meal, and the ones after that. Anticipating their moves was difficult, and the guide stayed busy repositioning the canoe to intercept.

Two anglers per boat, we stood back to back during these hatches, like lookouts, flies held at the ready, with enough line outside the tiptops to false-cast and shoot as quickly as possible. The tarpon angler or bonefisherman knows the drill. While it's helpful to be able to throw 90 feet, it's more important to be quick and accurate at only 40 or 50 feet. When the wind was down, the dorsal fins of the trout showed like landmarks, and if we threw the proper cast to the right spot with the correct fly, there was a small, pregnant eternity and then another awesome strike.

Although one memorable trout, on feeling the hook, immediately ran far into the backing and then snapped the leader with a long, barracuda-like leap (making even the guide shout), most of these fish fight down in the water, occasionally sounding to 30 feet in the deeper holes. Some were boated in 15 minutes, others took a good deal longer. All were carefully netted, weighed by hanging the net bag from the scale (rather than hooking a jaw or gill), revived if need be, and then released to carry on the species.

Between hatches, we prospected the shoreline and the creek mouths. Flinging a Muddler too close to a weed patch virtually guaranteed that a northern pike would come arrowing out of the shallows, often to clip the tippet and take the fly. Some of these Labrador crocodiles are big enough to attack even mature trout, sometimes leaving a survivor with tremendous scars on its back. The very largest trout, however, are safe from all predators but man and otter.

We spent one evening wading some very homelike stretches of fast water, and thereby found out where all the small (to 3 pounds or so) brook trout hang out. They are not completely safe even in the riffles and eddies, for as we strode through a tiny gravel pool between large boulders, I nearly stepped on a 2-foot pike with a 1-foot trout clamped crosswise in its jaws. The pike eyed me with suspicion and then, rather more hungry than frightened, swallowed the wriggling trout in three convulsive gulps.

Some of the best fishing is in the long northern evenings, after an excellent logging-camp supper and a gallon of coffee. The lakes are calm then, and the loons call. Later, after dark, when everyone has reassembled at the lodge, it's time for a wee dram and the day's stories—the time that often establishes the memories that we bring home from an adventure.

That week passed well. From the canoes, black Labrador rolled away in every direction under a classic northern sky—great clumps of cloud whose flat bottoms sweep to the horizon. When sunlight broke through, it was like a blessing and a smile.

Another successful transplant: a brook trout from the Green River in Utah. Tom Montgomery photograph.

A Quebec summer brook trout that struck a Bomber, a fly pattern meant for Atlantic salmon; the somber markings of this fish will soon change to the brilliant hues of spawning. Tim Leary photograph.

RAINBOW TROUT

GIVEN ITS STERLING qualities as a leaping, wild-fighting, predatory gamefish *plus* the fact that it is a true native, the rainbow trout, not the exotic brown, perhaps truly deserves the title of America's premier freshwater gamefish. A few anglers would be more specific and vote for the steelhead, the migratory lake- or sea-run race of rainbows that may grow to spectacular size and strength.

Rainbows are Westerners who were moved east, as well as all over the rest of the planet, including Europe, Africa, South America, New Zealand, Australia, and Japan. Unlike the American brook trout, rainbows "took" in many of those places, and have become as popular there as the immigrant brown trout have in America. And unlike most other salmonids, wild rainbows are generally spring-time spawners. They also cross-breed readily with other species (to the detriment of cutthroat trout in many Rocky Mountain watersheds), and of all the trouts they accept the widest range of water temperatures and quality. This makes the rainbow the darling of fish-culturists and has led to many hybrids and artificial sub-subspecies and hatchery experiments. The non-fishing public who see trout only on a plate, garnished with lemon and stuffed with . . . something, might recognize the rainbow; most frozen supermarket trout are 'bows, often reared, harvested and flash-frozen in Idaho or the Orient. And all over the United States, stream trout these days are often hatchery rainbows, pale cookie-cutter fish mass-produced and released annually to satisfy the increasing demands of the fishing public. It's a testament to the rainbow's style that even these fish usually strike a hook with a certain dash.

The trout's namesake is the slash of color that decorates its flanks. This may be a wide band of stunning hot pink, a pale rosy line, or simply an irregular boundary between zones of spots on the fish's back and sides. The rest of the fish may be deep green above, fading through yellow to a white belly, patterned with irregular black specks, or—particularly near salt water—blazing silver with hardly any specks at all. Rainbows can show remarkable variation from one river or lake to another, never mind from region to region and season to season, and there are dozens of different non-migratory strains, depending on how finely one draws the line. Among the better known of these subspecies are the redband trout of the Columbia River Basin and the Kamloops trout of British Columbia. Some rainbows migrate readily to open water such as lakes or even the sea, others remain resident in their rivers year-round. And the potential for tremendous growth is there too. Canadian fisheries biologists reportedly netted a Kamloops-strain rainbow of more than 52 pounds in Jewell Lake in British Columbia.

The most famous pure strain of rainbows is probably the McCloud River fish, of northern California. It was the eggs of this race that, beginning in 1877, were shipped so successfully to Australia, New Zealand, Europe, Japan, and the eastern United States.

It's not only the various types of arctic charr that still cause scientific headaches. The accessible rainbow, known and loved for generations, apparently hasn't been nailed down yet either. In the summer of 1988, the Committee on Names of Fishes, of the American Society of Ichthyologists & Herpetologists, voted formally to re-classify the rainbow. Weighing all the evidence, the fish would no longer be *Salmo gairdneri*; it was henceforth *Oncorhynchus mykiss*. What's in a name? Plenty.

It was a two-step process. First the rainbow was in effect declared an Asian fish. In its anatomy and genetic structure and in its behavior and habitat, the rainbow is identical to the trout of the Kamchatka Peninsula, that part of the Soviet Union that roughly parallels the Aleutian Peninsula on the other side of the Bering Sea. And since that fish has been *Salmo mykiss* longer than the American rainbow has been *S. gairdneri*, both would thereafter be *mykiss*. (Many animals—birds, walruses, polar bears, sea-going fish, even people—can cross so readily back and forth between Alaska and Siberia that they can only be the same.) That settled the question of species.

Next came genus, which boiled down to a sort of chicken-and-egg question: Is the American native rainbow a landlocked steelhead? Or is the steelhead a sea-run rainbow? The Committee decided on the former, which then made the rainbow "trout" officially a Pacific salmon. As a result, even native rainbows a thousand miles from salt water, who have never left their Montana streams,

The classic American rainbow trout; this one photographed by Christine Fong on Idaho's Silver Creek, itself a classic (and carefully maintained) trout stream.

now share the *Oncorhynchus* name with those migratory salmon. As do the hatchery rainbows that populate streams all the way east to New England. Fortunately, despite the ruling, the rainbow has not yet altered its genetic code to die after the first time it spawns, as the six "true" races of Pacific salmon do.

Names notwithstanding, the finest fishing for American stream rainbows is in a region where they live intimately, and depend upon, the Pacific salmon; in Alaska, where they're sometimes called . . . .

LEOPARD TROUT

"BIRCH CREEK" doesn't appear on any maps. It's a name the camp owners coined to try to keep the competition away from this river. It is on the southwestern coast of Alaska, toward the middle of Bristol Bay, and it gave me the best week of fishing in my life. This part of Alaska is famous for its big and plentiful rainbow trout, and for the incredible runs of salmon that come inshore to spawn from June to October.

In a remote camp, where roofs are canvas and the population is family-size, people, cooking and weather take on tremendous importance. All sunny days? No—but the odd day of cold rain spices up the Alaskan experience and makes the sun look so much finer when it does come out. Genial companions? Check. Hot and cold running water, and a shower? Check. Good, knowledgeable guides who also do a great Laurel-and-Hardy? A cook you'd like to bring home? Got it. Comfortable Beds? Heated tents? Transparent water? Vistas? It's all there.

From a float plane a thousand feet up and three miles away, the camp appears inconsequential—two brown and two green spots on a greener hillside next to a silver-blue river. In midsummer's low water, the plane has to land on a tundra pond on the far side of the hill, and the guides and a cook meet guests there, to help hump the gear over the path to camp.

Birch Creek Camp gets by with a pair of large quonset-type tents—one for cooking and dining, the other for guests—set on plywood floors. The fisherman's Alaska is right there, just outside the tent flaps. And the fish are right there too. With only four anglers in camp, morning prep time can be reduced considerably. Two fishermen and one guide per boat means that an hour after getting up you can be casting, even with a full and sociable breakfast under your wader belt.

Evenings, you sit on the cook tent stoop and count salmon (species and individuals) parading through the long, still pool below. Even in thigh-deep water, the big kings leave wakes behind as they bulldoze their way upstream. Others jump, for no apparent reason, sometimes three or four times in succession. Some say it's to dislodge sea lice, still riding piggyback from the ocean. But the lice die and fall off within hours of reaching fresh water; perhaps it's just that the fish, facing their life's journey and then death, are restless.

It was mid-July and so the dog salmon were already beginning to die. With their vertical, irregular red-on-green mottling they could be recognized as readily as the huge kings. The sockeyes, bigger than the dogs, smaller than the kings, were also going red, but with dark green heads. The pinks, the little humpback salmon, are still silvery-colored at that time. You couldn't see them from the stoop unless the light was just right. If you went to sit right down on the riverbank, then you could see humpies and cruising trout, occasional grayling and the metallic flash of Dolly Varden. These

A bull-nosed small rainbow breaks the surface of Wisconsin's Rush River. Photograph by Don Blegen.

waters hold seven kinds of gamefish at once; later in the summer, silver salmon, the coho, would swim up from the ocean.

The trout are the resident fish. When the salmon move into fresh water in great numbers, they may put the trout down for a few weeks. We were lucky; although the sea-run species were in, the rainbows were still actively taking our flies. They hadn't yet switched over to preferring salmon-egg imitations, as they do when the spawning runs are at their height later in the summer. The most effective "dry fly" this time was not an insect imitation at all, but a mouse—preferably large, scraggly, waterlogged, and tied with caribou hair. (It was all we had in camp.)

We fished these mice Western-style (or bass-style), casting from the center of the stream and banging them hard right onto the banks. Flop the mouse into the water, then skitter it away from

A native British Columbia Kamloops trout, showing the typical silvery colors of the lake-dwelling rainbow. Photograph by Christine Fong.

shore, using rod tip and current to make a surging wake. A flash underwater gave them away as the big rainbows bolted from their lies to give chase, sometimes missing again and again before con-necting with a violent strike. One hit five times on the same retrieve; another slapped the mouse with its tail and sent it spinning into the air before diving onto it. If a fish missed every time, we had only to rest it a few minutes, then go back for another series of wild charges. On the first day, we had to kill a trout that had been hooked deeply on a leech-pattern streamer. In its stomach were three tremendous lemmings. The Dolly Varden we took every day for shore lunch had almost all been eating tundra mice as well.

The rainbows were as alike as biscuits from the same tin. Most were 20 to 24 inches long, with vivid red streaks extending up onto their gills and cheeks, and vibrant black spots densely patterned

(above) A large Kamloops strain rainbow trout, photographed in British Columbia by David Lambroughton. Note the large red cheek blotch.

(right) A fabulously colored large rainbow trout caught in the Colorado River at Lee's Ferry, Arizona. Photograph by Christine Fong.

on their tails and bodies. Some call them Alaskan leopard trout, and the name is apt. They had the proportions and air of wild things that are well fed and ecologically secure; half-assed doesn't make the cut in Alaska. If our flies were mice, it was easy to think of the trout as cats—aggressive, graceful, sometimes almost playful. But predators above all, accomplished and deadly. They liked the springy caribou hair and would chew the fly and tug on it for long seconds after we tried to move it in their mouths to drive home the hook.

CUTTHROAT AND GOLDEN TROUT

THE MOUNTAIN TROUT, or cutthroat, is another North American native, a *Salmo* that, like the rainbow, exists in perhaps dozens of different strains, each seemingly more colorful than the last.

A small native rainbow still showing the parr marks of the immature fish along its sides. Photograph by Tim Leary.

Cutthroat trout, however, do not exist in nearly the same numbers that rainbows do; some are confined to a few small mountain lakes. Biologist Robert Smith, in his excellent *Native Trout of North America*, identifies 14 major subspecies of cutthroat—including the Snake River, Yellowstone, Westslope, Bonneville, and Rio Grande—and there are more yet. With this sort of diversity, the cutthroat's colors and size vary more than other salmonids, from yellowish-green to flaming red, with large or small, sparse or dense black spots; and a few races of deepwater cutthroat, such as the Lahontan cutt native to Nevada's Pyramid Lake, may grow to 40 pounds or more. Some along the West Coast, from southern Alaska and British Columbia to northern California, are anadromous. Cutthroat are desert as well as mountain trout, and distinctive strains of them were once found in the arid parts of inland Oregon down as far along the southern Rockies as northern New Mexico.

The visible common characteristic of cutthroat trout, the one from which the name derives, is a bright slash of red or orange along the lower jaw. (In some strains, the red slash may extend over a good deal of the fish's flanks, especially during spawning.) This jaw marking is present even in rainbow-cutthroat crosses, which are very plentiful in western U.S. rivers where the species intermingle. This easy hybridization frustrates salmonid purists, for some strains of cutthroat are among the most beautiful and rarest of trout.

As the desire to re-establish native races of fish gains strength in America, a number of western states have begun to breed and then plant their fish in remote—that is to say, undisturbed and safe—streams and lakes. Ironically, to make room for them, this often means poisoning out the other trout, rainbows or brookies or even lake trout, that were brought in to supplant the vanished

A fat rainbow whose ancestors, many generations back, were released as exotics into Vermont's Otter Creek. Photograph by Tim Leary.

A very western-looking but nevertheless eastern rainbow, caught and photographed and released in Pennsylvania's Fishing Creek by B&C Beck.

natives in an earlier "hatcherification." In more populated areas, this can actually cause a public uproar if the citizenry don't care to give up their "new" fish—and it's probably a good sign overall if even the general populace feels queasy about poisoning trout of any kind. Colorado's vivid green-back cutthroat are a good example. Remnant wild populations of them were found early in the 1970s in tiny mountain streams where they were protected from hybridization with other trout by waterfalls, impassable natural barriers. Their peers, the yellowfin cutthroat, had apparently gone the way of the passenger pigeon. Today, after much research into just how to rear them artificially and then release them into the wild, greenbacks are again propagating freely in Rocky Mountain National Park and the Roosevelt National Forest. They are still officially a "threatened" species and have not been released into unsupervised waters, but in 1987 Colorado opened a limited catch-and-

A predatory "leopard" rainbow, heavily spotted and silver-sided, caught in a small creek within a few hundred yards of the Bering Sea in Bristol Bay, Alaska.

release fishing season for them. The state is very proud of its unique resource, presently found nowhere else.

The golden trout, the state fish of California, was originally native to the Kern River basin of the Sierras, which the species had all to itself. Goldens, much like cutthroat and rainbows, cross-breed readily and thereby wipe themselves out as a strain; but, by the same token, in isolation they develop unique markings and other traits. To keep the biologists and taxonomists employed, there are at least three different strains of California goldens, each named for its watershed. Beginning in 1918, the golden trout was "hatcherified" and joined the long list of species that were being relocated all over the world. Its ova found suitable homes in Oregon, Washington, Idaho, Alberta and Montana, and down through Wyoming, Colorado, and Utah. Golden eggs were even tried in Eng-

A spectacularly marked 8-pound Alaskan rainbow caught feeding on salmon eggs well upstream from the Bering Sea. B&C Beck photograph.

(far right) Removing a caribou-hair mouse fly from the hard jaw of a "Birch Creek" Alaskan rainbow. The fish never came out of the water and was never handled; a single twist of the pliers removed the barbless hook with little or no damage to the fish.

A cutthroat trout from the Colorado River. Photograph by Andy Anderson.

land. But in 1939 California saw the light and made it illegal to export golden trout or their ova out of the state. Once 10-pound goldens were almost common in some mountain lakes, but now a fish two-thirds that size is a trophy. Goldens are apparently here to stay; although biologists say they have survived well at altitudes below 5,000 feet, today almost all golden populations are in lakes above 7,000 feet, and some a good deal higher, and thus more protected, than that. The Mexican golden trout, which entered the scientific literature only around 1960, has a bright orange belly and exists only in north-central Mexico between the Sierra Madre *Oriental* and *Occidental*. The relatively few fishermen who have added the golden to their life-list of salmonids have had to hike or horse-back into Wyoming's Wind River Mountains and other wilderness.

It is tempting to think that, unlike the eastern brook trout, trout of the Intermountain and Desert West have not had to face the same sort of overfishing at the hands of too many sportsmen (or even market fishermen), or industrial or agricultural pollution, or the ruin of their habitat as megalopolis expands. But that is not the case. The American West has been just as abused and overbuilt as the East (perhaps even more so, to judge by what happened to the Indian tribes, the bison, the plains grizzly, and so on). Native trout there have been dynamited for the table; poisoned by agricultural chemicals and animal waste; choked by silt and stressed by high temperatures as overgrazing stripped streamside vegetation and crumbled riverbanks away. And they have been, and are, one of the many mute losers in the West's interminable water wars, where local governments, developers, ranchers, and landowners all try to divide up free-flowing rivers for their own uses.

LAKE TROUT AND THE CHARRS

A CHARR is an arctic trout, a colder-water coldwater salmonid that is found around the world throughout the high northern latitudes. Charrs have light spots, while "true" trout—rainbows, browns, cutthroat—have black spots. Charrs are native occasionally as far south as about 40 degrees north latitude, and are found farther north than any other salmonid, including the huchen (see Asia) and other anadromous fish. Like their close relatives, the various charrs may be sea-run or land-locked, depending upon opportunity, genetic pre-disposition, and where the retreat of the last northern glaciation—roughly 10,000 years ago—stranded the forebears of today's stocks. In non-scientific terms, the arctic charr in northeastern North America parallels more or less the cutthroat in the West—bearing in mind that the cutthroats are *Salmos* and the charr *Salvelinus*, and that cutthroat occurred much farther south. (And while there are Western charrs, there are no native cutthroat in the East.) But like cutts, charrs are often wildly colorful, not so well known as other trout, regarded as fairly easy pickings by anglers, and the subject of endless hair-splitting by taxonomists. As with cutthroats, a few highly predatory races of charr grow to a very large size; and there are a number of distinct and highly localized races of charr (in northeastern North America and else-where), some of which haven't been seen for so long that they may be extinct.

There is, for example, a charr called the silver trout reputed to live in a single deep lake in the interior of Maine. A few specimens have been examined by biologists at the University, in Orono. The last one seen was taken by an ice fisherman around 1980, but since the lake can only be reached by hikers and access is controlled by a local public utility, the silver trout are probably liv-

A Westslope cutthroat photographed in Sutton Creek, near Florence, Oregon, by Don Blegen.

ing on unmolested. Other rare charrs of northern New England include the Sunapee and the blue-back trout, native to Maine's Rangeley Lakes, and there is a red trout in Quebec. Biologists have named at least 16 species of charr around the world, and more strains. There is even an Asian *fontinalis*, a subspecies that is not the same as the North American *fontinalis*, the brook trout.

Lake trout are also charr, unspectacular in color or behavior even though they are similar to huchen, with only their size to recommend them to fishermen. Of all American salmonids, the lake trout is regularly outgrown only by the Pacific chinook (king) salmon. In the Great Lakes, where these trout were an important commercial fish before the sea lampreys were introduced and drastically diminished the population in the 1960s, netters occasionally reported lake trout of 100 pounds or more, but a rod-and-reel fish of half that size is rare today even in the Northwest Territories.

Lake trout are widely distributed across almost all of Canada (where they're sometimes called gray trout), even well up into the Arctic islands, and from the coast of the mainland Maritime Provinces west into Alaska to Bristol Bay (the local name there is mackinaw). In the Lower 48, lake trout occur naturally only from northern New England (in Maine they're called togue) and upstate New York to the Great Lakes region. Lake trout have been transplanted, however, as far west and south as northern California.

Lake trout demand cold, clean water and they generally inhabit deep, well-oxygenated lakes with good smelt populations. They are the premier gamefish of the tremendous lakes of the Canadian shield—Great Bear, Great Slave, Athabaska and others—and anglers come from around the world to troll and cast for these huge, somewhat ponderous, wilderness predators. In warmer climates, lake

A lean and distinctly speckled Wind River, Wyoming, cutthroat photographed by Tom Montgomery.

The characteristic red throat slash of the cutthroat trout. Tom Montgomery photographed this fish also in the Wind River.

trout escape midsummer temperatures by living at depths of 100 feet—or much more.

Dolly Varden are charr of northwestern North America, found in great numbers, especially in the streams of Alaska and the Pacific Northwest that salmon return to for spawning. Like the coastal rainbow trout, Dollies feed voraciously on salmon eggs, and commercial fishermen claim they make sizable inroads into the salmon fingerling populations as well. These predatory habits help make them game fighters, and Dollies of 8 to 10 pounds are common, at least in less-fished drainages. Dolly Varden are as gaudy as any salmonid, with white-edged fins, blazing orange-yellow bellies and white- or even lavender-spotted sides and bronze-green backs. The story goes that these fish are named after Dolly Varden, a character in Charles Dickens' *Barnaby Rudge* who supposedly also wore lavender spots. However, research shows that Dolly's dress is described only as cherry-col-

ored. Another theory is that a northwestern gold-rush miner, who perhaps read Dickens by candle-light, romantically dubbed his claim "The Dolly Varden" Dolly being a popular Victorian name. These fish were undoubtedly in the stream nearby and perhaps picked up their name by association . . . . It's a long shot.

For over a century, the bull trout—sometimes known as the western brook trout—was commonly identified as a Dolly, even by fisheries biologists; the two are that similar in appearance and predatory feeding habits. But in 1978 a California scientist named Ted Cavender published his proof that the bull trout is a separate species. The fish is found throughout the Pacific Northwest, generally in big water—heavy rivers, deep pools, cold lakes. Positive identification of a bull trout versus a Dolly generally requires dissection in a laboratory, but here is the rule of thumb: In Northwestern waters

A typically marked and colored Yellowstone cutthroat, taken and photographed in the Yellowstone River in Montana by Tim Leary.

where both species might be found, any one that weighs much more than 12 pounds can safely be regarded as a bull trout.

In eastern Canada, arctic charr are often found in brook trout water, and fishermen who see only the spectacularly red-orange bellies and white-trimmed fins of both fish find them hard to tell apart. Arctic charr lack the worm-like black markings that brook trout carry on their backs; and while charr may be spotted, the spots are never surrounded by lighter halos.

Distinguishing arctic charr from Dolly Varden is another matter. The rule of thumb is that if the spots on the fish are smaller than the iris of its eyes, then it's a Dolly Varden. The western arctic charr generally also has a more forked tail. However, as their ranges overlap only from central Canada westward, it's generally safe to say that an eastern charr—taken in Labrador, let's say—is indeed a charr and not a Dolly. Certain identification may be much more difficult in Alaska and western Canada. I have seen obviously cross-bred charr in the streams of British Columbia's remote Cassiar Mountains that shared the characteristics of both strains.

The confusion among fishermen and disagreement among biologists over charrs worldwide started in the beginning. Carolus Linnaeus , the great Swedish scientist who developed the modern

(above) A 3 1/2-pound golden trout that has just been re-released into the Wind River in Wyoming. Photograph by Tom Montgomery.

(left) A Lahontan cutthroat caught from a float tube in a reservoir in Washington State. Darrel Martin photograph.

(above) Another, smaller Wind River golden trout by Tom Montgomery. The difference in color between an underwater fish and one in hand is startling.

(right) Salmo aguabonita, the golden trout. Originally native to the Kern River basin of California but transplanted throughout the Intermountain West. This large fish was photographed in the Bridger Wilderness of Montana by Tony Oswald.

way of classifying animals by genus, species, and subspecies, put his native Lapp charr into the wrong slot right at the outset, in 1758. He called it a *Salmo*.

STEELHEAD

IT WOULD BE AN easy mistake to regard Atlantic salmon as merely brown trout that decided to swim out to sea to grow up before coming ashore to spawn. There's a strong resemblance, barring vomerine teeth and subtle differences in body shape and markings, and both are of the genus *Salmo*: *S. trutta*, the salmon trout, and *S. salar*, salmon the leaper. However, they are not the same. A sea-run brown trout is called a sea-trout; a landlocked Atlantic salmon is still a salmon, not a brown trout. But in the case of the rainbow trout and its migratory kin the steelhead, no distinctions need to be made. They are one and the same—now *Oncorhynchus mykiss*. One goes to sea or into a large lake to grow up, the other remains in the river. The young of each (probably) follow their parents' example; and often both strains live—at least part of the time—side by side in the same streams. Most steelhead are fall- or winter-run fish, and the people who cast to them in their rivers must be prepared to deal with raw weather. There are, however, a few runs of summer steelhead as well. No one can say

A fly-caught lake trout from the George River, Province of Quebec. Photograph by Jerry Gibbs.

(far right) A large square-tailed Dolly Varden caught on an egg imitation during the salmon run near King Salmon, Alaska. The season is late fall, and the fish is in full spawning dress.

An Alaskan Dolly Varden in summer colors, photographed by the author in a tributary to Lake Iliamna.

what makes one fish decide to go to sea and another stay behind, but different strains are predisposed one way or another. McCloud River rainbows are generally stay-at-home types; consequently, there are few steelhead outside of North America, despite the vast numbers of rainbow trout (mostly McCloud) that have been introduced to other regions of the world.

In their original waters, steelhead are found along the western coast of North America from southern Alaska all the way down to Malibu Creek, just north of Los Angeles. Presently the run in Malibu is very small—a few dozen fish—and it is a wonder they can thread their way through all the craziness of the southern-California beaches. The local Trout Unlimited chapters have taken these fish under their protection, however, and are raising funds and public awareness to rehabilitate the spawning creek. Strong steelhead runs now also exist in the Great Lakes, from which the fish

A late-summer Alaskan Dolly Varden of the Lake Nunavaugaluk area, showing a local predilection for bright red. Photograph by Donna Williams.

swim up into rivers and streams from Minnesota to New York, and there are recognized steelhead as far east as Lake Champlain, on the Vermont-New York border.

Steelhead were named for their shining-bright chrome color at sea, and perhaps also for the blunt shape of the heads of particularly large fish. As spawning time nears, the silver color darkens and spots and the telltale red band of the rainbow begin to appear; in full riverine breeding dress, the steelhead is unmistakably a rainbow—if a large one. Every summer, steelhead of 30 pounds are caught and released again in the wild coastal rivers of British Columbia.

For North American fishermen, the parallel seems almost too neat. Atlantic salmon on the East Coast (generally) and steelhead trout on the West Coast (generally). Both are oversize versions of beloved stream trout; both offer the angler, particularly the fly fisherman, a superb challenge. Therefore an experienced salmon fisherman should be able to head West and succeed famously with the steelhead, and vice versa. But it ain't necessarily so, despite the broad similarities. These two fish do not respond the same way. Steelhead are migratory, often anadromous, but—like sea-trout (and the Pacific salmon they in fact are) and unlike Atlantic salmon—they are not locked into spawning in only one river, the river of their birth. Steelhead tend to follow their noses and each other,

(above) A charr, possibly a bull trout, from Racetrack Creek, near Deer Lodge, Montana. Photograph by Don Blegen.

(left) The typically fine spots and silvery sides of a sea-feeding Dolly Varden caught in an estuary on the Bering Sea.

An eastern Arctic charr taken in a tributary of Ungava Bay in northern Quebec. Photograph by Adriano Manocchia.

swimming up into fresh water more or less along the lines of least resistance. It is the Atlantic salmon that is the renowned homebody, and this may account for the differences in the way these two great trophies are fished for. Seemingly every Atlantic salmon river has its preferred fly patterns and its specific angling techniques, and they often work better than any other flies or methods. Is this because the local experts tell us it is so and, believing them, we fish that way confidently and therefore successfully? Or could it be that after dozens or hundreds of generations of salmon have returned to *this* river to see *that* fly and *that* technique, the fish are conditioned to respond to them? And does it then also follow that steelhead fishing is much the same within each broad region be-cause those fish do not always return to exactly the same water, and so do not develop such stream-specific likes and dislikes?

Then again, maybe this is all horsefeathers. It is true, however, that Atlantic salmon generally prefer flies or lures that travel quickly, while steelheaders are forever manipulating their lines to slow down the progress of their lures through the water. Both species are at home in fast water, but the steelhead goes on feeding when it has left the sea or lake, while the salmon absolutely does not—sometimes for as long as nine months. Its metabolism has changed, diverting energy from the

A large Dolly Varden being released back into Alaska's Beaver Creek. Photograph by Andy Anderson.

A formation of Arctic charr hovering in the crystal water of Umiakovik Lake, Labrador. Photograph by Gilbert van Ryckevorsel.

digestive organs to the sexual organs.

SALMON

THE SALMONS are anadromous fish, which simply means that they swim up rivers from the sea at certain seasons to lay their eggs. In this simple sentence is the essence of a salmon, the key to what distinguishes it so remarkably from its close relatives, the trout and charr. Like most of them, the salmon is born in a riverbed and passes its juvenile years in fresh water, but then some force as mysterious as the one that brought its parents upriver originally prompts it to swim downstream and out into the salt. This is the beginning of the salmon's great life-and-death migration. The young smolts mature into salmon at sea, traveling freely to feed upon limitless herring, eels, capelin, and shrimp.

Barring encounters with commercial fishermen (who may or may not be looking for them, but may sweep them up as "bycatch" in the pursuit of something else), sharks, big cod and a few other predators, life is grand out in the open ocean. The fish may gain a pound a month. There's room to roam, and little to cramp this fish's bold style. But in two or three more years, or five or six for some individuals, an age-old hunger draws the salmon out of the infinite, safe ocean deeps and sets them upon a journey few will survive, despite their now-prodigious size and strength. The need to spawn, to reproduce the species, to keep the eternal cycle going, urges the salmon toward shore. How? It is thought they navigate according to oceanic currents, the earth's magnetic field, and perhaps even the positions of the stars.

In coastal waters, relying on a sense of smell/taste far keener than any scientific instrument yet

Steelhead flies from the Great Lakes rivers, photographed by Larry Dech.

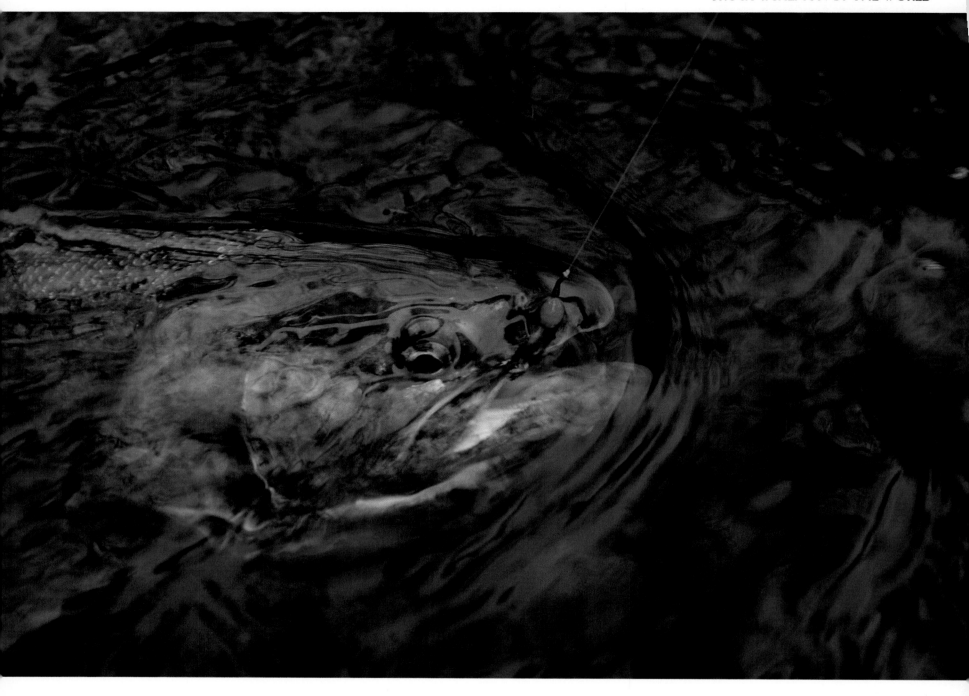

(above) A steelhead of the Pere Marquette River, a tributary of Lake Michigan. Photograph by Larry Dech.

(right) A large, chrome-bright, fresh steelhead from the Bulkley River in British Columbia. Photograph by David Lambroughton.

built by man, salmon home in on minute traces of fresh river water mingling with the sea. When they enter the estuaries their troubles begin. As the coast begins to embrace the salmon within its headlands, the seals increase. Even small fishing boats find them easily and badger the schools with their nets. Along the shore wait elaborate stake nets, weirs, fish wheels and other traps. Then in the river mouths the bottom shoals rapidly, and even hungry birds can now reach the fish, though only an already injured salmon can fall prey to a bird at this stage. The salmon that survive pass up into the still-narrower confines of their rivers and streams. In Europe, they are finally relatively safe, except from man. In North America, the natural predation begins in earnest for otters, mink, fisher cats, ospreys and eagles. In the Northwestern United States and Canada, the grizzlies have been waiting for the salmon to appear ever since they emerged from their winter dens. And man is there

too, waiting with his dip nets, spears, lures and flies.

Little wonder then that the salmon—grown extravagantly strong in the wide sea, now hemmed in by stream banks; forced to thread swift currents and negotiate rapids, rocks and shallows; unable to eat; and diverted from the spawning imperative by predators of every sort—becomes a tiger on rod and line, a champion battler for freedom. The saltwater wanderer becomes a freshwater gamefish without a peer.

On the Atlantic coast of North America, the salmon is *Salmo salar*, the leaper. This beautiful, large fish was once so common from Ungava Bay down to about the Delaware River that early colonists wrote of killing spawning salmon simply by riding a horse through the stream. Their home rivers have been dammed and spoiled and the fish stocks reduced by netting to the point where Atlantic salmon have become a prized catch. River clean-up and ever-stricter regulation of all types of fishing on both sides of the Atlantic have halted the salmon's long decline, but it will never be as common as it once was. And even these mighty efforts may be wasted if acid precipitation is allowed to continue. Atlantic salmon grow to prodigious sizes in Norway. In Maritime Canada, a few rivers produce a 40-pound fish nearly every season, but 10 to 25 pounds is the norm; farther south, in Maine's Penobscot River, 10 to 15 pounds is a good fish. Every Atlantic salmon river also has an annual run of grilse, smaller salmon (variously defined as under 24 inches, or less than 10 pounds) that are thought to be sexually immature.

Unlike the Pacific salmons, Atlantic salmon do not necessarily die after spawning. As water flow and temperatures permit, small bands of salmon struggle "home" sometimes winning their way a hundred miles or more upstream until they reach a pool with the right combination of current and substrate. The hen fish selects a spot and, holding herself almost flat to the bottom, sends the gravel flying with powerful strokes of her broad tail. With the aid of the current she soon has scoured out a large, shallow redd, or nest, in which she deposits her eggs. The male fish (having driven off rival suitors) takes his turn, fertilizing the eggs with a cloud of milt, and then the hen goes back to work, covering the eggs with new gravel she digs from just upstream. In so doing, she creates another redd and often uses that as well, eventually laying some 7,000 to 20,000 eggs.

The Atlantic salmon stay in the river through the subsequent winter and return to the sea, if at all, in spring. Then they are known as kelts, or black salmon. Nearly starved, still facing upriver as though heeding the echo of the spawning urge, they allow the spring currents to push them back to the sea. Something on this journey—the smell of salt water?—triggers their feeding habits and once again they begin to eat and grow, regain their strength perhaps to return a year and a half later. It is estimated that only some 5 to 10 percent of Atlantic salmon survive predation and injury to spawn a second time. Very few accomplish this three and even four times. The salmon young, first called parr, pass their first two or three years in the river until, as smolts of maybe 8 inches, they too head for the salt.

The landlocked salmon of New England and eastern Canada (where it is called *ouananiche*) is an important gamefish also. Biologically and physically it is the same as its now-larger sea-run relative, a streamlined torpedo with the same greeny-black back and small black X's scattered across its silver sides. The original "landlocks" were cut off from the sea by some glacial accident and learned to

This steelhead in northern California's Mad River is beginning to show the spawning rainbow slash of its tribe. Christine Fong photograph.

substitute a lake for the salt water, and to swim upstream into a tributary in the fall to lay their eggs. After the last glacier retreated from northeastern North America, 6,000 to 10,000 years ago, these freshwater salmon were established in Labrador and Newfoundland and as far inland as Lake Ontario. Overfishing, pollution, dams, and destruction of their habitat shrank the range of the landlock to Maine and eastern Canada, where they remain. Today a 5-pounder is rare, but a salmon of more than 22 pounds was taken from Maine's Sebago Lake in 1907. The state of Maine, aware of the value of its landlocked salmon, began to propagate the species for sale as far back as 1868, and virtually all the landlocked salmon that have been transplanted around the United States and the rest of the world were Sebago fish. In America Sebago salmon transplants are living as far west as Michigan; elsewhere, they caught on extremely well in southern Argentina and Chile, where currently the biggest landlocks in the world are found.

FOR CENTURIES the feeding grounds of the salmon were a mystery, but in time the secret inevitably came out. In the Atlantic, Danish and Canadian netters found them off Greenland and the Faroe Islands, while Japanese and Korean fishing boats homed in on Pacific salmon (and steelhead) in the great basin between North America and Asia. Ever since, politicians and fisheries biologists and sportsmen and commercial fishermen on all sides have been embroiled in controversy.

The Atlantic salmon, though not as plentiful, may actually be the less threatened at the moment, thanks to the spread of salmon aquaculture. The days when servants petitioned their masters, in Europe and in America, not to serve them salmon more than three times a week have been long gone; salmon is a delicacy, costly if no longer rare. Now, due to various market pressures, only one Atlantic salmon in ten served at the table is a wild, net-caught fish; the other nine were all reared in a pen anchored in salt water somewhere—Maine, New Brunswick, Iceland, Norway, Ireland, and elsewhere. Various governments, from Canada to Scandinavia, have also begun to ban near-shore netting of returning salmon because anglers have been raising such a howl about it. No, it hasn't been the howling that persuaded the politicians; rather, it is the enormous sums of money injected into local economies by these anglers, who often hail from elsewhere and pay freely for the privilege of casting to salmon. Money talks, and salmon walk. Now (early 1990) talks are underway among sportsmen to simply buy up the annual Atlantic-salmon catch quotas still allowed by international agreement to the commercial fishermen of Greenland and the Faroe Islands, who are the most active remaining high-seas salmon harvesters.

Commercial fishing interests are far stronger in the Pacific, however, and the salmon runs are far greater in variety, geography, and numbers of individual fish. There seems to be enough to go around for both commercial and sports fishermen, but many private groups and government agencies in Canada and America watch these runs with the intensity of ospreys. And all groups become enraged when Asian boats intercept the migratory fleets at sea, inside or outside the 200-mile fishery zone. At stake is even more than the sportsmen's pleasure and dollars, and the livelihoods of American salmon packers, brokers, and commercial fishermen. The entire coastal ecologies of the northwestern United States and Canada depend unequivocally upon these salmon and the billions of eggs they deposit every summer. Increasingly, however, the voice of the sportsman is being

An immense (27 pounds) steelhead caught and released in British Columbia's legendary Babine River. By its deep colors, the fish has been in fresh water for some weeks. Tom Montgomery photograph.

heard, and his money is beginning to "talk."

ON THE PACIFIC COAST from Monterey, California, north to the Bering Strait there are five distinct species of salmon, all in the genus *Oncorhynchus*. Like *Salmo salar* in the East, they migrate every summer from the sea into freshwater rivers and streams to lay their eggs. Unlike the Atlantic fish, these salmon do not return unerringly to their birth rivers; nor do they ever survive the spawn. After rapidly changing from the shining silver they wear at sea to various unearthly shades of red and dark green, every one of the millions of these salmon dies in its river.

Each of these five salmons has at least two different names, depending on the region and who is speaking of them. The largest, least plentiful, and most valuable (for market and for sport) is the

chinook, which may exceed 5 feet in length and reach a 125 pounds in weight. Certain Indian tribes know the fish as quinnat (a name that stuck when chinooks were successfully transplanted to New Zealand); in British Columbia they may be called tyee. But in the far Northwest, it's no surprise these fish are known as . . .

Pink—or humpback—salmon, still silver from the sea, moving steadily upstream in a tributary of the Fraser River, British Columbia, to seek spawning sites. Photograph by Michel Roggo.

ALASKAN KINGS

ON THE VERY first night in camp I encountered the two biggest fish I've ever seen in fresh water. Later, it took on the surreal quality of a dream.

Primed for a week in the Alaskan bush, brimming with the enthusiasm of new arrivals, we three sports had plunged into Birch Creek Straightaway after supper and fairly jitterbugged through the

Male Fraser River sockeye salmon: his deep red color, green head, and good condition, indicate he probably has not spawned yet, but will do so very soon. Photograph by Michel Roggo.

pools near camp. We were *here*, this is *it* ! *Alaska*, man! Adrenaline can work miracles but, like the northern twilight, it eventually seeps away. By midnight, jet lag had surpassed all other considerations, and I was letting the current guide my steps back downstream to the tents.

In a bouldery run no wider than a moderate cast and hemmed in by rock walls, I met the fish, a mating pair of king salmon. I entered the chute from upstream; the two torpedoes swam up from below. Even in the subarctic dusk, I could see their wakes. As the water shallowed, their dorsals and then their backs and tails broke the surface. They pushed up over the first gravel bar, dropped into a narrow channel of deeper water, and then spotted me watching them. The spawning urge must have been on them; there stood a bear-sized creature in the stream, yet they shot towards me, then veered off for an end run.

My first impulse, I admit, was to let them by. There wasn't much room, and the smaller one looked to be 50 pounds. His girlfriend was the scary one—if he was 50, she had to go 75 or better. Two years before, farther south along the Bering coast, a mere 17-pound king had crashed into me while trying to throw a hook, and nearly toppled me sunny-side down. This pair looked like they could break legs. But I gathered my courage—*They're just aiming to get by, not attacking*—and shuffled to block them off. They feinted; I followed. They hung back to wait. I felt almost as trapped, in the top of the run, as they were; we were in checkmate.

Weariness was gone. I was charged up. I shook out line and began to work a streamer past their noses. It was unlikely they would strike in such a situation, but maybe one would be aggressive enough to overcome its fears. And I'd never know unless I tried. In the gloom, and with a genuine case of buck fever, a good cast was no easy matter. The two salmon simply ignored the fly; it twitched off by them and then, to my annoyance, was hit hard by a lurking rainbow. Only in Alaska can an angler be frustrated and peeved by the inadvertent strike of a 4-pound trout. And only in Alaska can an angler sight-fish to such champions as this pair of amorous battlewagons.

The salmon had enough and retreated back into deeper, wider water. The cigar shapes were there one second, gone the next. I gathered up my line and waddled on home, by now almost staggering. I couldn't have endured an hour or two of frantic fish-fighting then anyway.

The dogs—chum salmon—were beginning to die. They were there in the greatest numbers, and while every day we caught chums that were still vigorous, every morning we found fresh carcasses washed up on the gravel bars. Then the swifter deterioration began; the eyes went first, to gulls and ravens. If a larger animal didn't drag the whole thing away, then insects began tunneling in and, a few days later, all that remained were skin and skeleton, like a deflated salmon balloon.

By the end of the week, the dogs were dying more noticeably, around our feet, while we watched. Ancient-looking fish would appear, grey and greasy yellow, bony-jawed, literally in tatters, spawned out but still struggling to answer the call to swim upstream. Anal fins and lower tail were invariably gone, wasted by the fish's inability to eat and then scraped away by a hundred passages over rocks and riffles. Each spawned-out salmon eventually reached a chute somewhere in the river where the current was too much. The fish would die there, repeatedly and ever more slowly swimming up and being repulsed until it turned turtle and drifted away, finally headed downstream. While the pools around us bloomed with the vee-wakes of living, hungry, feeding and spawning fish, the downside of the cycle was there too. Life into death, death into life—couplings in a food chain older than the river itself.

Although the countryside is tundra, the waterway and its sediments support small trees, and the hills break enough of the wind to let them grow. Consequently there's firewood, deadfalls and driftwood bleached by the sun. The guides beached the skiffs while we fished on, and soon they were working over a cooking-bed of red coals. The entrée was fillet of Dolly Varden, sautéed and served with skillet-fried onions and potatoes. As an appetizer, perhaps a mug of chicken soup, a by-product of last night's supper; for side dishes, rolls and butter, canned corn or green beans. And for dessert, toll-house cookies (big ones, baked the evening before, with lots of chocolate chips and brown sugar to make then chewy), pastry, carrot cake. There was cowboy coffee and cans of soda

Summer-run Atlantic salmon nosing into the flow of the West Branch of the St. Mary's River in Nova Scotia. Photograph by Gilbert van Ryckevorsel.

and even beer. My waders seemed to shrink daily.

In the evenings, the excitement of the day supports you just long enough to stow the gear and get into camp clothes. While supper cooked, there was time to watch the river over the rim of a glass. (Yes, there was ice in the gas-fired refrigerator-freezer). At northern latitudes, evenings last for hours. Coffee, dessert, diary-keeping, tackle-mending, fly-tying, conversation, a game of Trivial Pursuit, and even more fishing, for those whose day went by too quickly. With bed and board 40 feet from the river's edge, post-prandial angling is only a matter of a minute's walk and hardly requires the attendance of a guide. It was safe; although we saw fresh signs daily, bears generally shied away from camp, and the noise of the outboards in the morning cleared them out of the river.

In midweek we traveled downstream several miles to where the river forked out and braided into

A pod of returning Atlantic salmon holding on the bottom of the upper Salmon River in Fundy National Park, Nova Scotia, photographed by Gilbert van Ryckevorsel.

channels, and fished roaring little sluices and still, deep holes and brushy cutbacks. Regularly, a trout came charging out from the overhangs, its open mouth showing white in the green water, to slaughter a mouse-pattern fly. The day began dark, clammy and cold, but by mid-morning the fog had burned away and the sun shone on us. The fishing improved as the sun climbed.

Eventually we arrived at a long, straight pool with a beach on one shore and a high bank on the other. There were ghostly reddish shapes hovering in the depths of the center channel. Other salmon passed by in the shallower water, and behind them swam grayling and Dolly Varden and rainbows, waiting for spawning to begin and the protein-rich eggs that would drift downstream. It was too early for the kings to spawn, and we could see none of the sofa-sized redds they build. I waded in at the upstream end and began to drift a fly, low and slow, through the herd. A dramatic

hit—too enthusiastic to be a big salmon, too red to be trout. It was a jack, an immature king, of about 5 pounds. A few more casts and then there was a very solid strike and a great commotion out in the middle of the pool. This was 20 pounds of king salmon, a handsome, red-bronze creature that tore up and down for 20 minutes before consenting to be handled, photographed and released.

The others went on downstream. Andy, one of the guides, stayed with me while I worked the pool some more. In an hour, I hit and immediately lost two of the big salmon. Their takes were almost imperceptible—fly and line simply stopped in the water. Each time I reared back hard, preferring to lose a fish at the outset instead of after an hour's labor. Both fish came right away to the surface, thrashed, and were gone. I had to sit and recover after each one.

Then we went into a dry spell. Andy and I worked up and down the hole for half an hour. Finally we went back for a last try in a narrow slot where dozens of kings had passed while we ate, sometimes churning the water like outboard motors. From a cast away upstream, I could see new fish there. I quartered the fly across current, let it sink, and monitored its progress into the top of the slot. I lost sight of the fly. Then there was a solid pull and I was fast to a huge salmon. His head broke out of the water and then a tail like a shovel came up and splashed water into the trees. Andy

(above) A healthy and typically marked Sebago-strain landlocked salmon from Maine. Photograph by Tim Leary.

(left) A Great Lakes chinook salmon comes to the net. Doug Stamm photograph.

An Atlantic salmon parr, showing its characteristic vertical bars, that was released in New Hampshire's Pemigewasset River as part of the extensive salmon restoration program in the Northeastern U.S. Tim Leary photograph.

and I screamed; the fish took off downstream. Andy ran to push the boat off and follow.

In waders, I could cross and re-cross the river. Although the salmon took more than a hundred yards of line right away, I had plenty left and it was unlikely this big ocean fish would intentionally tangle me in the brush along the cutbank. The leader was short and stout. The various connections had been tested and proven. Preferring to lose the fish sooner than later, I put everything I could against him, tried to snub the fish while reeling myself downstream, but in reality I reeled and ran.

It was half a mile of river before we caught up with the fish and the others. Birch Creek flowed out of the woods into another, longer pool, with a broad beach on one side. The salmon had breached five times now—elephantine thrashings that turned my knees to jelly and made me shout. At the top of the new pool, I threw him some slack and ran down the beach. Without the goad of the line,

he made his only mistake: He stopped running for the sea, and let me get below him. Now I could hold him into the current, make him fight me and the river. When he turned downstream, I moved through the crotch-deep water to cut him off. When he sulked, immovable, on the sandy bottom, I slapped the bowed rod on the water and shuffled towards him until he broke and ran away. He was beaten, if I could hold on.

I rehearsed what I would do and say when the hook pulled free. Alternately I decided I'd be cool and philosophical or furious and determined to try again. Miraculously, it wasn't necessary. After an hour and a half, the salmon swung around me into a downstream arc and let himself be beached. Both guides fell on him. The others cocked their cameras. I stared and let my arms stretch out.

We had no scale large enough to weigh such a fish. He was 4 feet long, probably 55 pounds. I

A large male Atlantic salmon hiding in the brush on the bottom of Nova Scotia's East River. Photograph by Gilbert van Ryckevorsel.

The Grande Cascapedia River on Quebec's Gaspé Peninsula is a famous big-fish Atlantic salmon river. This solitary cock is still moving upstream. Photograph by Gilbert van Ryckevorsel.

knelt in the shallows with him, cradled and coddled him. I wanted him to go back and breed lots of new salmon who would also look favorably upon fishermen's flies. He was happy to oblige. For the rest of the week, I sported a saucer-sized bruise under my sternum from the rod butt.

Saturday, usually the last day in a fishing camp, came up foggy and cold and still, but by 10 a.m. it was again blue and warm. Sarah, the chef, joined us and the whole party slowly moved upstream, looking for new fish and experiences to end the week with. We were relaxed and jovial, appreciative of everything—the crystalline water and sandy bottom, last scraps of fog turned to silver by the sun, the line of rocky scarp against the deep blue sky. We all knew it had been an unusual time.

By early afternoon we'd floated back to camp. Gear was strewn everywhere; waders draped over the tents to dry, rod tubes came out from under bunks, flies plucked from hats and vests returned to

A spawning pair of Atlantic salmon resting on their redd under an embankment in the East River of Nova Scotia. Gilbert van Ryckevorsel photograph.

their boxes. The three who were leaving appeared, one by one, in travel clothes outlandish and formal after a week in sweat pants and wool shirts. An airplane materialized, with four strangers on board, and so began our journey back to the rat race.

THEY ARE NOT ACCEPTED as "real" gamefish, but three of the other four Pacific salmons nevertheless give the angler a decent thrash on rod and reel. Humpback salmon—known also as pinks—are relatively small, slab-sided, with almost beak-like jaws and strongly humped shoulders. They are first-class table fare when fresh and bright, especially for campers who need a break from Spam. Chum salmon, whose other name, as noted, is dog salmon (because the native people of Alaska and Canada netted them to feed their dogs in winter), are more plentiful in the lower rivers of western Canada and Alaska. They are bigger than humpies, generally 10 to 15 pounds or so, and do not turn

(far left) A pod of Atlantic salmon in Silver's Pool, the St. Mary's River, Nova Scotia. Note the lone sucker at the bottom. Gilbert van Ryckevorsel photograph.

Proper technique for releasing Atlantic salmon to live on. This 25-pound cock fish was taken in the Margaree River in Nova Scotia, photograph by Gilbert van Ryckevorsel.

(above) An incredible Atlantic salmon caught—and released—in New Brunswick's Restigouche River in 1988 by Mike Crosby of Halifax, Nova Scotia. By comparison to the canoe ribs, the fish measured 31 inches from the tip of the nose to the center of the dorsal fin; according to biologists, this made the fish's overall length a stunning 60 to 62 inches, and thus set its weight at approximately 65 pounds.

(right) Pacific chum salmon about to be released back into a stream feeding Bristol Bay in southwest Alaska. The fish, a male, has not spawned yet and its fins are only beginning to show the wear and tear of swimming over countless gravel bars on its long freshwater migration.

A pair of sea-bright silver salmon caught in a fork of the Goodnews River near the Bering Sea in Alaska's Bristol Bay drainage. David Lambroughton photograph.

crimson to spawn. Instead they develop startling streaks of maroon that extend up their green sides like dull flames licking at a board. In spite of their reputation as "dogs" they will take lures and flies and fight for their survival, at least while still fresh.

The sockeye, or red, or kokanee salmon is the most plentiful in the Northwest. Found from San Francisco on up the coast to Bristol Bay, it's the one most likely to show up on the label of a can of salmon. It is no trophy even when fresh, but it can be spurred into striking a hook. The sockeye's chief benefit to sportfishermen (and to hunters, netters, conservationists, and anyone else interested in preserving the Northwestern ecology) is the sheer size of the annual spawning run. Those millions of fish and the billions of eggs they lay every summer are the prime food source for many other gamefish, and for other animals ranging from insects on up through birds and foxes to the

A fresh Alaskan pink, or humpback, salmon destined for the table.

coastal grizzlies.

Though much smaller than the chinook, the coho, the fifth Pacific salmon, gets the vote as number one gamefish from many anglers. Its reputation as a hook-and-line battler (and the ease with which it can be relocated) has led to its transplantation into the Great Lakes and waters as far east as Lake Champlain. Cohos are now found even in a few coastal New England rivers, and there is a move afoot by the state of New Jersey to plant cohos in the mouth of the Delaware River. Even fishermen who respect this salmon as a gamefish are aghast at the idea, for the Delaware, especially in its upper reaches, is perhaps the finest wild-trout river system in the East. The coho would probably displace the trout, disrupt their spawning patterns, and perhaps even introduce new diseases.

In its native northwestern rivers the coho is often known as the silver salmon, a name that suits it

The author's 50-pound king salmon.

(above) The teeth of a chum salmon would do credit to any fur-bearing carnivore. The author photographed this spawned-out male seconds after its death.

(right) The carcasses of spawned-out salmon litter thousands of miles of shoreline every fall in the Pacific Northwest. The fish and their eggs keep more than their own species alive; they are a critical link in the food chain that affects all animals, from microorganisms to brown bears.

well. Whether in the estuaries or newly arrived in fresh water, these fish are chrome-plated beauties with speed and strength. Silvers are extremely valuable fish, for they bring millions of dollars of sportfishing revenue into their regions. Even in the most distant corners of Alaska, new ways of life based upon the salmon are emerging . . . .

SILVERS

IN 1971, the Alaska Native Claims Settlement Act (ANCSA), formally re-established Alaskan Indians and Eskimos and Aleuts as landowners, and in effect made Wall Streeters out of them too. The U.S. government handed these native people more than $800 million in cash and title to, eventually, some 44 million acres of Alaska. Thirteen regional native corporations were set up to administer this property, and, through smaller member corporations organized in towns and villages, all beneficiaries of ANCSA became stockholders.

Anxious in part to treat the Alaskans with a humanity that was spectacularly lacking a century before, when the Plains Indians were getting their lives reapportioned, the federal government decided to allow two full decades for these new ventures to get to their fiscal feet. It was acknowledged that

the natives would likely hire white businessmen and attorneys to advise them. But to ensure that con artists would not descend on the fledgling corporations, and their fabulous holdings, like grizzlies upon the spring moose calves, ANCSA stipulated that the natives could not sell their stock to outsiders for 20 years. In 20 years, it was reasoned, solid investments would have been made, native boards of directors would gain the experience to compete on a par in the marketplace, and stockholders in general would become savvy enough to resist the blandishments of takeover artists. The natives were given land (prime land, this time), plenty of money (in 1971 dollars, at that) and time—all the ingredients, it was thought, to cook up a new native culture, one that would let them have muktuk *or* Big Macs, whichever they wanted. It was, many felt, a bold and generous plan.

Now, 1991 is here, and while some of the 13 regional corporations have done well, others are in much worse shape than when they were founded. Many of the satellite corporations are going broke, either by their own actions or because of poor investments by their regional. And the fastest way for a company—particularly one with hard assets—to raise cash is by selling stock. It's possible that control of much of Alaska will once again pass out of the hands of its native people.

What these past 20 years, however, have shown to Alaskans, both white and native, is that canned salmon, crab, gold, timber, fur and particularly oil are not the dependable income producers they once were. Tourism, on the other hand, and its twin, recreation, are strong and becoming stronger. Alaska still has incomparable wilderness and animals and fish; everyone knows it and nearly everyone wants to see. Part of those 44 million acres of ANCSA land could conceivably become the world's largest sportfishing, hunting, canoeing, hiking and nature-photography preserve.

This is how the silver salmon comes to play a major role in the politics of Alaskan land use, for one of the most spectacular of the native corporations' attempts to lure sportsmen's dollars is a fishing destination called White Mountain Lodge. White Mountain Lodge was brand-new in 1987, designed by a California architect and built and staffed by Eskimos. It is in the native village of White Mountain—population 150, more or less—which is about 80 miles east of storied Nome. Both lodge and village are on the banks of the Fish River, which flows clear and clean into Norton Sound, an arm of the Bering Sea just below the Arctic Circle. Although some individuals herd reindeer or prospect for gold, the White Mountain people hunt, fish and trap to get by. The lodge is the White Mountain Corporation's business venture.

A fishing lodge, however, is more than a business proposition. A fishing lodge is where business bumps head-on into fun, and where business and conservation interests coincide directly, for once. Fortunately, White Mountain's fishing is good. But if you're emotionally involved with Alaska's rainbow trout, White Mountain isn't for you. Because there aren't any rainbows in the Fish River; it's too far north. The Kanektok River is generally regarded as the northern edge of the Alaskan rainbow's range, and the Fish River is about 300 miles farther north yet. So no trout. But the Pacific salmon, particularly the silvers, appear there dependably (and one can even get a crack at the mysterious sheefish, which—it's only fair—don't live down in trout country).

In a country brimful of rivers with wonderful, sonorous, exotic names like *Agulowak, Kanektok, Tik-Chik, Kuskokwim, Nushagak* and so on, why is this one called the *Fish?* Poetry it's not, but then again the name is apt, for the Fish is full of fish. The Seward Peninsula has been home to several thousand

Inupiak Eskimos for some thirty centuries. It didn't take them long to discover which neighborhoods were best for fishing. The river they chose for their summer home, where they fished for themselves and their dogs, would naturally become known as the fish river. When white missionaries arrived there, only about three generations ago, they stamped out the native language as part of their meddling. Presumably then the fish river's "real" name was translated into the Fish River.

UPON unfolding oneself from a small plane after arriving on the dirt strip at White Mountain, a visitor notes two things: a horizon-girdling panorama of river and tundra stretching away to the ocean southward, and, much closer at hand, the village burying ground, which abuts the airfield. A surreptitious check reveals no crosses with inscriptions relating to aviation accidents, so the visitor continues his stroll to the edge of the bluff and looks down onto the village of White Mountain. Below, in the hollow between this hill and the next one (which is the real White Mountain), and arranged along a gentle bend of the river, are a few dozen small buildings. There are many boats lined up on the beach. A couple of satellite dish antennas jump up out of the scene. On the dirt streets looping back and forth and around everything red beetles are scurrying—the three- and four-wheel all-terrain scooters that have become basic summer transportation in the Arctic.

Turning to the north, the visitor notes the river flowing in long arcs down out of the distant hills inland. Miles away, but easily seen in this pure air, a speck is drawing a dark scratch across the silver ribbon of water—a skiff hurrying back to camp, maybe with a load of net salmon.

Mid-August is already early fall up here; still about 22 hours of daylight, but that decreases rapidly. The king salmon have turned red and retired in pairs to the tiny feeder streams upriver, spawning in secrecy. The fishing now is for silver and chum salmon, and the odd humpback, as well as charr, grayling and northern pike.

The first fishing morning dawned gray and very cold. It's always a small surprise to learn again just how much clothing it can take to be comfortable on an Arctic August day. But cold is partly psychosomatic. We could see the trailing edge of the overcast advancing by us, moving up from the ocean. By noon we were fishing under a friendly blue sky. The temperature climbed a bit and our spirits improved even more—no more coffee breaks in the boat; now we were fishing in earnest, Polaroid glasses on, wet to the waist, blood pressure elevated just a tad. And the fish began to come.

My boat-mate, Fred, knew how to catch silver salmon. He spotted every hidey-hole, every current break where experience told him the salmon should be, and he worked his flashy streamer with confidence. He got three, bang-bang-bang, so fresh and bright it almost hurt to look at them in the sun, while I dredged up a few small charr. I was not too proud to stalk into a hole he just vacated and toss out my own tinsel streamer, on a sinking line and with a lead-core braided leader, to boot. A good swing in the current, the fly now well below the surface, a few energetic strips, and wham! The line jumped from my stiff fingers. The salmon surged back and forth, but I reined him in and forced him up. The fish thrashed out into the air, and I got the surprise of the day—this salmon was dark, and had a huge flag of a dorsal fin! It was a grayling, but what a grayling! A grayling with shoulders and a grim look in its eye. When I got it in hand, it was a fish for the IGFA record book. I measured it, and guessed 4 1/2 pounds, knowing that a 24-inch, late-summer trout, for example,

often weighs 5 pounds. And so there was my fish story for that trip—caught, inspected and released on the first day.

The Fish River is some of the most wadable big water in Alaska. Its current is placid, there are no rapids at all and hardly any riffles, and the bottom is comfortable gravel or sand. And, at the village, the Fish *is* big, maybe as much as 200 yards wide. But it's not very deep, and in normal conditions a 6-foot fisherman could probably wade clear across it in some places. Whatever the depth, the water is almost as clear as the air; skimming along in a boat made me think of some Arctic version of a tropical bonefish flat. Every stone, every log, every fish was suspended in its element below us. Upstream, the river narrows progressively, and its character changes. Tributaries of all sizes pour in, some big enough for boats, and every one is a new angling opportunity.

The fishing is excellent, with many fish, large fish and lots of room for them to run. But what sets this place apart is, unquestionably, the Eskimo presence. There are fish camps up and down the river, and boats from White Mountain and two other villages (Golovnin, on the salt water, and Council, up on the tributary Niukluk, where a huge gold strike occurred in the first years of the 20th century) pass by. But their presence is not intrusive. It's not the same as finding another lodge's boat in a pool ahead of you, or seeing the commercial fishermen come upriver in their 32-footers when the nets are slow, as happens down in Bristol Bay. The Fish River people live there, and have lived there far longer than our families have been in North America. Like the moose, the bears, the seals and the salmon themselves, the Eskimos belong.

Occasionally, villagers joined guests for dinner at the lodge. By the second bottle of wine, these meals began to resemble friendly press conferences, with guests firing question after question at the natives. One can imagine that after a busy summer or two, the duty of meeting-the-guests could become tiresome:

"Here, it's your turn to go eat at the lodge."

"Oh, no! I did it Tuesday; you're up."

"But I'll go nuts if I have to explain how we hunt seals again!"

"So tell them about the bear that busted up your camp yesterday."

Seventy-three-year-old Tom Brown told a group one evening about his adventures down in the Lower 48. In 1946, he and his wife and two children visited the Eastern states with a traveling Arctic show—with their furs and tools and weapons, they were the live Eskimo diorama. Their third child, a son, was born then, in New Jersey. Tom remembered that winter in Boston as terrible, bitingly cold and damp, and how pleased they all were to come back home to White Mountain again.

Out on the river, one of the most picturesque camps, on a point at the confluence of the Fish and Niukluk Rivers, belonged to Percy Agloinga and his wife. Both elderly, they were hale and hearty. Percy shouldered his huge wooden whaleboat off the beach and into the water with little apparent effort. When we first stopped there, he was gutting out a netful of chum salmon, working with a butcher knife on a scarred table with its legs standing in the river. The wooden planks were bright with red-orange skeins of roe and slabs of salmon. A battered ulu lay nearby, the half-moon blade that is traditionally a woman's knife. A rifle leaned at hand, in case a moose should wander by. Beyond were Percy's white wall tents, strung together by laundry lines, and well-worn paths and a

Silver salmon drying on the rack at an Eskimo camp on the Fish River near White Mountain, Alaska.

fish-drying rack with a gull's wing scarecrow dangling from one pole. By their dens in the riverbank, each chained to a stake, Percy's 13 sled dogs dozed in the sun. There were few working teams left in that country. Percy used his primarily for trapping. He said he prefers dogs to a snowmobile because the machine contaminates the trapline with the stench of gas, which scares away the animals. (Karl Ashenfelter, chairman of the White Mountain Corporation board, also traps, but he used a snowmobile. Dogs, he says, smell up the trapline too much and scare away the animals . . . .)

On our last day we stopped our skiffs at a bend, the river so wide there was almost no current on the far side. Silver salmon, 8 to 10 or 12 pounds, swam slowly along both banks, resting after the 40 miles they'd traveled up from the salt. We began to take fish. Hookups came in twos and threes; the fish were played, lost or landed, and then that spot of water went quiet. The pods of fish moved, but never far. A few steps up or down the bank, a few exploratory casts—shorter usually worked better than longer—and we were back into them. They came in all colors, from silver to flaming red and every shade in between, and all fought hard. It was playtime, and we called back and forth across the river, struck heroic poses for each other's cameras, fished side-by-side with the guides.

Nothing left to prove. Time to ponder some questions. Such as: Can sportfishing flourish alongside subsistence fishing, on the same river system? Yes, at least here. The White Mountain people net for their own needs, not for sale elsewhere, and their fish harvest diminished greatly as snow machines replaced dogs. (A dozen dogs eat 4 to 5 tons of dried fish annually.) And in recent years moose have arrived on the Seward Peninsula, which further reduces the natives' reliance on salmon. There are no tremendous fish traps blocking whole tributaries; most people use only 50-foot nets, and seines at that, which don't kill the way gillnets do. It's common for a one-man seine operation to release alive half the fish in a haul that's too big to deal with. Overall, natives take only a very small part of the annual Fish River salmon run.

At this writing, it is too early to say whether White Mountain Lodge will flourish. The economics of travel, sportfishing, and venture capitalism all intrude severely upon the project. Regardless, the lodge and the salmon have set an example for others in Alaska—an example that will be ever more valuable in 1991, the pivotal year for the native corporations.

Not the same fish but it could be, two weeks later: A Fish River silver salmon that is about to be released so it may complete its spawn before dying.

South America

THAT TROUT AND SALMON exist at all below the equator is a tribute to our meddling with ecosystems. As industrial man fanned out of Europe in all directions after the Dark Ages, one wilderness and one aboriginal people after another fell before his hunger, his diseases, his ships that could sail upwind, and his iron weapons and iron discipline. Not surprisingly, wherever he went as a colonizer in the centuries to come, he found the land could stand some "improvement" some change that would make it more homelike. Home-style architecture, clothing, religion, language, cooking, and even recreation followed him around the globe, to ease the chores of subjugation.

The British, bless their imperialist hearts, did more to spread their sort of fishing and shooting sports than probably any other group of people. In Victorian times and earlier, with a disregard for (perhaps a lack of understanding of) regional ecosystems that would be appalling in today's more enlightened society, British military men and commercial travelers and fortune-seekers—those who spent long periods of time away from the homeland—transplanted "their" trout and salmon (and gamebirds and stag and so on) over much of the earth. While assuring ourselves that we would never be so ecologically insensitive, at least now, we heave a sigh of relief that they were, and guiltlessly enjoy the fruits of their labors in many corners of the planet. In actuality, it seems they generally did more good than harm, at least with coldwater gamefish.

Nowhere is this eco-meddling more astonishing than in the Southern Hemisphere, which developed, biologically speaking, rather separately from the Northern Hemisphere. Part of the reason is the simple isolation of some of the land masses (such as Australia) in the vast Pacific Basin. And part is the equator, the "heat belt" that has never been glaciated, at least since the age of mammals began,

which has made it impossible for many cold-loving animals from higher latitudes to migrate north or south across the world's middle. Europeans stocked Patagonia, Australia, New Zealand, and the Falkland Islands with sheep and cattle, to take advantage of (among other things) the fact that either the heat belt or simple isolation had kept bears, wolves, large cats, and other major predators penned up in their hemisphere or on their own continents. Along with the crop animals, to these places were brought European and—in the case of Australia, New Zealand and Patagonia—American trout and salmon. (A few indigenous carnivores, the Tasmanian wolf for example, were eventually hunted down and extinguished. Australia's dingo dogs survive despite the best efforts of ranchers. Other predators, such as the foxes and condors of the pampas, are no great threat. Outside of Africa, the big predators of the Southern Hemisphere all seem to live in the water—sharks, orcas, crocodiles and so on.)

Today, as more and more fishermen are learning to appreciate native (as opposed to exotic or hatchery) trout, it is ironic to realize that none of the salmonids' anglers who travel so far and at such great expense to cast to in the Southern Hemisphere are "natural"—not a one. There is also a certain irony in the fact that these transplanted gamefish not only thrived in these new waters, they in fact outdid their peers back home. The Southern Hemisphere is far less populated and polluted than the Northern; the various strains of Atlantic salmon, brook trout, rainbow trout, and brown trout that made the trip down there (in the holds of square-riggers and motor vessels) took to those clean and uncrowded watersheds with gusto. Their transplantation has been called an "ecological miracle." They filled what seemed to be a true natural vacuum and, on balance, certainly contributed more to their new environment than they took away.

Today, the brown and rainbow trout fisheries of New Zealand's crystalline lakes and streams are perhaps the best of their kind on earth. Same goes for the sea-trout of far southern Patagonia and the Falklands.

PATAGONIA: *Cultured Wilderness*

WHILE THERE ARE transplanted brown and rainbow trout in the highlands of tropical South America—in Bolivia, Peru, Ecuador, Colombia, and Venezuela, salmonids are most at home in Argentina and Chile. These countries periodically rattle their sabers at each other across their common Andean mountain border, but both trout and salmon took to the rivers and lakes on both sides with the fervor of converts. The Rio Colorado, which cuts across Argentina about 200 miles south of Buenos Aires, is the northern boundary of Patagonia, a vast wilderness area that encompasses the entire tip of South America. Patagonia is dotted with towns and even a few cities, and it is home to some of the largest ranches and most hospitable people on earth. A thin network of gravel roads link its corners. Commercial fishing boats work its shores, and there are oil rigs down around the Strait of Magellan and even modern factories near Cape Horn. But Patagonia is wilderness, with unnamed mountains and rivers, harsh weather, wildlife that does not fear man, and pure air that is tonic to the lungs.

The region is also dotted with large lakes, each of which has a system of rivers and streams flowing into and out of it, and each becomes a salmonid fishery unto itself. Until recently, conservation

A wild rainbow trout from the Arroyo Pescado, a unique spring creek near Esquel, in the Andean foothills of Argentina.

A wild brown trout from the Rio Grande in Chubut Province, Argentina.

was unknown, but there were comparatively very few anglers to kill the fish. In 1988, however, the angling aristocracy of Argentina banded together in the Federation of Fly Fishers devoted to expanding the country's network of protected waters and to establishing an American-style catch-and-release ethic. Fittingly, as it was an American outdoor writer, the late Joe Brooks, who introduced fly-fishing for trout to Argentina in the 1950s. Today, his memory is even more revered there than it is in the United States.

The chemistry, flow rates, bottom composition and temperature of Patagonia's waters generally favor not only salmonids but also the food organisms they live on. On both sides of the Andes, along with good aquatic insect hatches and native baitfish populations, one of the reasons trout have flourished is the *pancora*, a freshwater crab that is an important food source. It's been said that,

as trout habitat, Patagonian rivers can hardly be improved upon. There aren't even (again) any predators to attack the trout, although this changes abruptly when the sea-run fish venture into their estuaries, where seals, orcas, cormorants, and penguins wait.

Brown trout were introduced to Chile from Germany (or England, depending upon who tells the story) in 1905, and English browns reached Argentina in the same decade. Ten years later rainbow trout arrived. Thereafter, fish were moved around from watershed to watershed seemingly overnight. The history of these events is not as well documented as it was in Australia, for example. This was not the colony of a European nation with an outdoor press already in place, and on the large and distant *estancias* in this wild region there were a number of private plantings. However, in 1903 a fish hatchery was built at San Carlos de Bariloche, 850 miles from Buenos Aires in the Ar-

A Rio Grande rainbow trout, bright as any steelhead but 300 miles from the Argentine coast. Compare the color of this trout with the rainbow from the Arroyo Pescado, only a few miles away.

A fantastic rainbow, grown fat on pancora crab, of the Rio Traful. The angler is Carlos Sanchez, noted Argentine angling guide. Photograph by Charlie Meyers.

(above) Another salmonid for which Argentina's Rio Traful has become famous—the landlocked salmon, originally stocked from Maine. Richard Franklin photograph.

(right) The North American brook trout has prospered in the cold streams of Patagonia. Photograph by Richard Franklin.

gentine Andes, and nearby Lago Nahuel Huapí, an ocean of a mountain lake, served as a nursery for those early releases of brown and then American rainbow trout. (Much as Lake Taupo did in New Zealand.) The world-record 35-pound, 15-ounce brown trout was caught in the lake in 1952. Near Bariloche is the Rio Traful, which became the original home of landlocked salmon in South America. The story goes that the salmon fry (more of the ubiquitous strain from Sebago Lake in Maine) were being transported to Bariloche by mule cart—the railroad did not yet extend that far—but the trip took longer than anticipated and the fish finally had to be dumped into the nearest available water before the heat killed them. That was the Traful, which even today is regarded as the finest landlocked-salmon stream on earth, even though the average size of the catch has dropped considerably in the last 40 years. Landlocks are also found in southern Chile now, and both countries have

(above) A stunning chrome-plated Chilean rainbow from that country's Rio Pescado (a common name throughout South America, it just means "fishing river"). Photograph by Carolyn Roth.

(right) A round-bodied 8-pound sea-trout from the Kau-Tapen water of the Rio Grande on Tierra del Fuego.

another exotic from the state of Maine as well—*Salvelinus fontinalis*, the brook trout. They have adapted so well that today the biggest fish rival the 8- to 10-pounders of northeastern Canada's large lakes.

Atlantic salmon from Britain were released in Tierra del Fuego and reportedly on the Chilean side of the cordillera as well, but as has always happened south of the equator, they swam to sea and were never seen again. Pacific coho salmon, however, have reportedly taken root in southern Chile.

TIERRA DEL FUEGO... AND OF SEA-TROUT

IN THE LAND OF FIRE, sheep now is king—sheep and the microchip. The Indians, who lit the fires (probably warning beacons) that Capt. Ferdinand Magellan saw that autumn evening in the

Another, very similar sea-trout, one that may be even more recently arrived from the South Atlantic.

year 1520, as his ships entered the strait that King Charles V later named after him, are gone, victims of imported diseases and repeating rifles. They began to vanish from Tierra del Fuego in 1580, the year two of them were grabbed, christened—"Francisco" and "Juan"—and taken as souvenirs to the Spanish court. There were no trout.

Across the big island of Tierra del Fuego and the inhabited parts of the accompanying South Atlantic Islands, which is to say in an area the size of Vermont, there were living at least four distinct tribes of natives when Magellan "discovered" the place. (Tierra del Fuego and Magellan's strait show up on maps dating back to about a century after the birth of Christ.) Two tribes were guanaco-hunting inland nomads; two were sea Indians, also highly nomadic, who hunted from bark canoes for otters, fish, seals and birds. Like their counterparts throughout the rest of the Americas, they were to receive the combined benefits of missionary zeal and colonial expansionism.

If all this seems to be yesterday's news, consider this: While the Haush tribe has been extinct for some years, and a few dozen Yahgans and Alacalufs reportedly still live, the last pure-blood Ona Indian in Tierra del Fuego died only in 1969. This isn't merely dry history—it's happening today. Jacqueline des las Carreras, née Menendez, the gracious lady who invited me to fish at her family's Kau-Tapen Lodge, on Tierra del Fuego, is a direct descendant of one of the families that established a stronghold there around 1900. About 20 years later, it was John Goodall, manager of the family's meat-packing plant on their estancia, who planted brown trout in the Rio Grande, which flows east through the ranch from the Andes to the Atlantic. As much as we frown on fooling around with Mother Nature, most of us will admit Goodall did good-all. Most English and Scandinavian experts now consider this the finest known sea-run brown trout fishery.

For the 1986-87 season—summer in the Southern Ocean—the Kau-Tapen log shows that 35 fishermen landed and released 217 sea-trout averaging 4.2 kilos (9 1/4 pounds); fish under one kilo were not recorded. The following summer, in seven weeks 27 rods landed and released 425 sea-trout whose weight averaged just over 8 pounds. The largest fish of the period was a 20-pounder, and half a dozen 17- and 18-pound trout were taken.

Other aspects of recent history affected the sportfishing there as well. The bloody government put-down of a miners' revolt in Rio Gallegos, north of the Strait, in 1921, reaffirmed the control of the big landowners over the countryside. And the equally short, savage, and even more bloody Falklands/Malvinas War had the unlikely effect of bringing industrialization to Tierra del Fuego. The Argentine government declared its portion of the island (west of the Andes belongs to Chile) a tax-free zone. The town of Rio Grande, at the mouth of the river, now boasts electronics and other assembly plants belonging to Sharp, Grundig, Hitachi, Casio, Massey-Ferguson and others. Before the war the town had about 15,000 inhabitants. Five years later, the population had swelled to 50,000. This is a frontier; environmental protection ranks somewhere below earning a living and staying warm. Household trash is dumped by the truckload directly onto the beach. On weekends all these new citizens need recreation—trout fishing, for example. The incidence of poaching—unsanctioned fishing on the Rio Grande—is up (comparatively; it is hardly noticeable by European or American standards). Virtually the whole river, 100 kilometers or so, lies within but five estancias, and public and private interests are in conflict again.

Kau-Tapen ("fishing house" in one of the Indian tongues), 45 miles outside of town, has about 25 kilometers of river, and even a full complement of a dozen rods couldn't cover every pool completely in one week. In low or medium water, the river is a picnic to fish—an endless series of endless, linked bends. The faster, fish-holding water is on the outside of each bend, the good wading is on the inside, and rarely are the two more than a long flycast apart. There's no waterfall or rapids, few riffles, and scarcely a tree; the fierce Antipodean wind is nature's axe. The river bottom is lovely, uniform gravel, and to a non-biologist's eye, the Rio Grande seems ideal spawning ground, with miles and miles of comfortable waterbeds for trout.

The river is a picnic to fish except when the wind is up, which it nearly always is. But to everyone's amazement, the wind hardly blew during my stay at Kau-Tapen. The residents tried to rattle me with tales of winds that peel back car doors and roll sheep like tumbleweeds, but they never materialized. These latitudes are the "Howling 50s" the bane of mariners, nastier even than the "Roaring 40s" just to the north. One of the many benefits of having 25 kilometers of river to fish, however, is that one should always be able to find pools situated just right for good roll-casting.

It's the last week of March 1987. Fall in the Southern Hemisphere; late fall, in fact, way down here. (Ushuaia, the southernmost town in the world, is about 70 kilometers over the hill.) Kau-Tapen is as far below the equator as Goose Bay, Labrador, is above it. This would be October, up on the Minipi. The des las Carreras family, who own and operate the huge sheep ranch of which the lodge is a part, are packing to leave when I do, to spend the winter in semi-tropical Buenos Aires. There is frost at dawn—about 7 A.M., here and now—but by late morning the sun has burned through the ground fog and all is gold and blue and warm. The fishing comes in the transitions, when the mist is half gone, the sunlight half on the stream. There's an hour or two of real excitement then, which dies down when full sun strikes the water. These are brown trout, after all, typically night-feeders in the rest of the world. But all is not lost; there is a sit-down, multi-course luncheon awaiting us back at base. No streamside, eat-in-your-waders sandwichfest here.

Conforming to the ethic that fishermen and hunters aren't happy unless they are uncomfortable, we faithfully got out early and stayed out late, bumping back in the evenings over the rutted road with dust hanging in the headlight beams. But the trout came mostly in that two-hour interval in late morning.

They are brown trout, yes, but this is salmon fishing—wet flies quartered down and across the stream, on short tippets and lead-core braided leaders and maybe even sinking-tip lines as well. To my great pleasure and fortune, my companion, Kau-Tapen's head guide that season, is none other than Stockholm's own Roland Holmberg, who has helped me take big fish elsewhere. He knows sea-trout (and Atlantic salmon) as well as anyone, and he is the best stream-fishing guide I know.

Cast-and-step, heave-and-go or not, this is demanding fishing because everything has to be right in order to fool these wary trout. It is more demanding than salmon fishing. The artificial fly you show a Fuegian trout may be the first it has ever seen, but that doesn't mean the fish is going to be a patsy. In Europe at least, sea-trout are extremely long-lived; Hugh Falkus writes of individuals who have returned to fresh water to spawn more than a dozen times. (Maybe 1 percent of Atlantic salmon survive to spawn five times.) Does that sound like a fish given to rash strikes at unfamiliar things in the water? It is amazing what is *not* known about these Fuegian trout, though. The spawning run starts in November, when the males begin the arrive, but at the end of March we were still catching fresh silver and ready-to-spawn colored individuals. Some fish appear to have been in the river a whole year, yet no one has yet reported catching a spawned-out hen fish. No one knows just where their redds are, either—they're "upstream somewhere." To confuse matters even further, locals say that in the Rio Gallegos, a hundred miles up the coast, the biggest fish are not the migratory individuals but the stay-at-homes, and claim they get just as big. Argentina does not provide government biologists.

You can't see them, but you must nevertheless stalk the fish. Roland is always after me to move quietly, cast quietly, put the line down gently, pick it up smoothly, speak softly. He peers over my

Far smaller and more colored than its silvery sea-run relatives, this Rio Grande brown trout is a year-round resident fish.

shoulder. Cast more upstream; add line and cast more down-angle, right to the bank; mend up, mend down; more fly speed, less fly speed. Let it swing in the current. Strip, strip. Work the rod tip. It sounds like guide-talk, making the fishing seem tougher and the guide smarter, but I know Roland and he knows he doesn't have to bullshit me. When I do what he says, the fish come—one even to a skating dry fly. The 3-, 4-, and 5-pounders are little rockets. The big ones, ready to calve, are slower and more ponderous this late in the season, but awesomely powerful. They thrash on top like king salmon twice their size. The strikes, on submerged Woolly Buggers and the like, are unseen but definitely felt—sometimes violent, never hesitant—and then the fish turns for the salt. Like Baltic sea-trout, these grow fat on herring and have characteristically small heads and blunt, heavy bodies.

The land is severely beautiful, lonely and wild. Not as dry as the American Southwest, but with

the promise of punishing winters. It is part New Mexico, with sheep and a pencil-line of fence reaching to the horizon, and part pre-bush plane coastal Alaska—tundra-like, with gravel beaches, high cutbanks, a broad expanse of blue or dull-silver water flowing smoothly toward a line of low hills. Bristol Bay could be just beyond. On one horizon the Andes loom, bright with snow and sharp edges. Fishemen/birders are particularly delighted here—Avian life goes from hummingbirds on up. At the coast are albatross and petrel and penguin; in the sheep country inland there are thousands of Magellan's and upland geese, mustering now to migrate (northward!) for the winter. Condors soar overhead on great wings, scanning for carcasses. Blocky ibis stalk among the manure piles, poking for grubs. Tufted cara-caras, peregrines, and other hawks quarrel over carrion. In sheltered shallows are flocks of flamingos ducking for snails and other delicacies. Bunches of elegant guanacos appear sometimes, woolly wild llama-cousins that look like they weighed 300 or 400 pounds. They haven't been hunted for generations and have little fear of man. And everywhere there are handsome gray Patagonian foxes, trotting industriously to and fro.

The meat-eaters are all here because of the transplanted sheep, cattle, horses, and rabbits. A few cormorants move upriver from the coast, following the alien trout. There's talk of again trying to in-troduce the Atlantic salmon. Everything looks natural and almost wild, almost deserted, but in fact little is as it was before Western man arrived.

Journal entry:

7:15 p.m. Sitting on a stone beach in bright, golden sun and a hard wind. Warm, though I've left my sweater and oiled coat in the Peugeot, with the tea thermos, half a mile away. We're exploring new water (not difficult with 25 km to choose from). No fish landed and I lost a big one an hour ago, after lots of elephantine thrashing, when the hook pulled out. I'm resting after fishing 100m of cutbank with wind and sun directly in my face. I can drive the line out OK but the wind pushes the big fly on its tippet straight back. So you fish the lulls and the angles, slide the fly in there with every intuitive trick you can muster, and the result is at least satisfaction, if not fish: a job done as well as you can.

As the sun sinks, the sky flames vividly and then it gets cold. Across the river, a silhouetted guanaco suddenly laughs hysterically at me and moves away to feed.

THE FALKLAND ISLANDS: *The Search Continues*

SEVENTEEN HOURS OUT OF ENGLAND, with one hour still to go on this interminable flight, the clouds beneath us thicken ominously and fill in from horizon to horizon—which is a hell of a spread, when you're six miles up—and I begin to worry. The Falkland Islands have a bad reputation for weather as it is, and we may just have to turn around and go all that way back to Ascension Is-land, to wait and try to get in again later. Ascension, at this point, is seven hours behind us. England eight hours north of that. Boston eight hours farther still. My eyes are bloodshot and scratchy, the brain is fogged, the stomach insulted by two days of airline food. I want to land so bad I'm thinking about a parachute if the plane does get waved off.

Shortly thereafter Squadron Leader Hoyle comes on the tannoy (this *is* a British—Royal Air Force, in fact—aircraft) to announce that "the weather in Mount Pleasant is generally fine, with bits of rain. And also snow and sleet. Temperature is on the cool side—6 degrees Centigrade. We'll be joined shortly by an escort of Phantoms doing practice, so don't be alarmed when you see them on

The same 17-pound sea-trout, a dark hen fish gravid with her eggs and ready to spawn. Roland Holmberg photograph.

the wingtips." A bit later he warned us about high winds ahead, noting for our cheer that we would have a turbulent landing and that the weather was keeping the Phantoms from lifting off to join us.

Actually, I *am* cheered, as it seems we will be landing after all. I want to get out of this thing soooo baaaad. Damn the weather, full speed ahead. And rolling Phantoms, I recall, are notoriously tender in even wimpy crosswinds. In fact the landing was almost an anticlimax. Squadron Leader Hoyle is no greenhorn, it seems, for he brought that hulking big jet down through savage gusts and lashing rain literally without a bump. We were on the tarmac and rolling with no sensation of landing. Top-class service from the folks who won the Battle of Britain . . . and the Battle for the Falklands.

The Battle of Britain was six years ago, but the Tristar taxies into a sea of military olive drab. The ground crew and baggage handlers are decked out in olive drab. The small crowd gathered in the blowing rain to meet us were dressed in sports camouflage, rakish berets, field jackets and those ribbed sweaters with the shoulder pads, beloved of American mail-order houses, that evidently really are British military surplus. All that's visible through the mist and wrack (if you can't use that Hardyesque term in the Falkland Islands, I don't know where it would be appropriate) is olive drab also—motor-pool Land-Rovers and busses, a couple of armored cars, an entire village of prefab clusterhuts, including the terminal building itself. All this and that fighter escort that was grounded—is Argentina about to try again? Hey, I'm just a fisherman looking for a few sea-trout . . . .

As opposed to Tierra del Fuego, trout arrived in the Falklands considerably later than Queen Victoria's Day. According to Bill Luxton, who runs the sheep farm and has a small lodge at Chartres Settlement, and who was there at the time, a milk churn full of English brown trout was dumped into the Old House Stream in 1954. The browns proceeded to eat the local "trout" which weren't trout at all, but rather a small and somewhat mysterious semi-salmonid classified as *Aplochiton zebra*, and then they disappeared.

Oh, well—easy come, easy go. Four years later, however, the locals began to notice these big, handsome, flashy, silver torpedoes thrashing about in the Chartres River, which the Old House Stream feeds. A few forays with rod and reel showed that, sure enough, those original few *Salmo trutta*, brown trout, had swum out to sea, prospered mightily and returned, when their spawning clocks went off, as *Salmo trutta*, sea-trout.

Fortunately sea-trout are promiscuous where their natal rivers are concerned. Unlike Atlantic salmon they will enter and spawn in any old (clean) stream, tending simply to follow each other and the currents and to avoid obstacles. Thus, with maybe a little help from farmers longing for something besides mutton or upland goose on the table, sea-trout soon spread to most of the other major rivers of the Falklands. I say "most" because no one I spoke with could absolutely vouch for their presence in every stream.

If that sounds as odd to you as it does to a visiting angler, consider that the 5,000 square miles of the Falklands—about the size of Connecticut—are inhabited by only 2,000 people. (Not counting the new-since-'82 military garrison of another 1,900.) The Falkland Islands Angling Club, based in Stanley, where half the population lives, has about 40 members. Of those, according to club president Terry Spruce, only a dozen are active. Statistically, sportfishing hardly exists here. Some streams go several years between visits by *any* humans, fishermen or shepherds or stray naturalists.

There is an "if" that looms large in angling here—the one that says the fishing is good if the trout are running. There's little doubt about that. The iffy part is so important here—much more than in Alaska, let's say, or even in Iceland, or other places where sea-run fish play a big part—because the streams are otherwise empty if the trout are not in. There are no fall-back species to cast to if one misses the spawning run—no big rainbows, no grayling or northerns. Not even whitefish. Just the occasional runty resident *trutta* whose forebears couldn't muster the *genitalia* to go to sea and grow up. Nor is there another run of some salmon. Falklanders planted Atlantics at least once, which swam out to sea and never returned (just as in Tierra del Fuego, 350 miles to the west).

The key to Falklands fly-fishing, then, is to hit that five- or six-week spawning window just right, which means juggling the calendar, the weather and the water height to arrive in the right spot at

A young British Army captain shows off a brace of sea-trout from the Green Hills Stream, near Port Howard on West Falkland.

the right time. No easy task, as any angler who's ever traveled more than 300 miles from home to fish can verify. We've all heard that we "oughta been here last week." This time, thanks to some mysterious delay that put the trip off three weeks, into late April, it was "you shoulda been here *three* weeks ago." We did find many fish, but it took a while. We also found very pleasant people, an un-expectedly beautiful landscape and, courtesy of the *Fuerza Aerea Argentina*, some unusual souvenirs. And penguins.

The Falklands are an archipelago of some 200 islands. Some are mere rock outcrops; two, East Falkland and West Falkland, are thousands of square miles each, separated by Falkland Sound, which is about 12 miles across. Despite the sophistication of the sheep business and the now twice-weekly flights from Britain, this is highly undeveloped country. The only paved roads are in Stan-ley. The only "high-speed" motorway, graveled and hemmed by nasty ditches and looking as if the Alaska Highway before it was paved, runs about 50 miles along the east shore of East Falkland, from Stanley to the new Mount Pleasant Airport and beyond.

We Rovered up and down that road for a few days to fish the Frying Pan River and Swan Inlet—"we" being three Brits, a Norwegian and a Dutchman, and myself. (I was the one in the red jacket and blue neoprene waist-waders, an outfit that goggled the Barbour-and-Wellies crowd.) Our sport there was pleasant but only that. We found no big trout—4 pounds was tops. The upper Frying Pan, narrow and splashy between rocky pools, offered us plenty of lively, bright trout, but they were about a foot long. Hardly worth traveling halfway around the world for. *Shoulda been there three weeks earlier.* We got to spend a few days in Stanley, though, and any visit to the Falklands naturally begins and ends there.

Stanley is a pleasantly basic community of small homes arrayed in rows on the hillside parallel to Port Stanley, the sheltered harbor. On the other shore, picked out in white rocks, are the names of British warships that were stationed there in lifetimes past—Protector, Barracouta, Beagle, and others. When I saw it, the harbor held the hulks of several 19th-century sailing ships, a couple of Korean squid-fishing boats, in for repairs or to rotate crews, and three small, somewhat battered cruising and yachts. In the streets and the few bars and restaurants, the small hotels and shops, the new military hospital, the locals are easy to pick out. They wear rugged woolens and walk purpose-fully or drive Land-Rovers. The soldiers are easy to pick out too, of course. They look shockingly young to me, but then we're not used to soldiers in the streets of America. The few foreigners, jour-nalists or commercial fishermen, engineers, salesmen or consultants, speak English with a varying degree of ease and carry sample cases and Halliburtons, and newspapers and magazines from all over the world. There's a trickle of such people through the bank, exchanging currencies. (The Falkland pound equals the British.) They give Stanley some of the international hustle of an oil-drilling or mining outpost, but one that is much cleaner and more homelike than most.

Out at Port Howard, West Falkland, the grass strip is smooth but contoured like a roller coaster. But the orange windsock was still, the airplane had been rock-steady throughout the hop over Falk-land Sound from Stanley, and the nattily uniformed young pilot oozed confidence. He pirouetted the government air service Islander twin on its starboard wingtip and slid rapidly down toward the landing strip, catching it on the crest of a swell like a surfer with a wave. Bumpbump—touchdown, mown grass blurring by the lowslung windows. The plane flew clumsily into the trough of the runway, then drove up the other side, halting gently on top. A Land-Rover drew alongside.

Robin Lee was at the wheel, smiling and taciturn. He had come to pick us up for his Port Howard Lodge. It's only a few hundred yards away, the congenial white house visible from the edge of the airstrip hill. A breath of smoke shows from its chimney; throughout the inhabited Falklands, the tang of smoldering peat drifts in the air. In April, the season here at 51°20' South Latitude is autumn, and the air is chilly.

As settlements here go, Port Howard is not small—about 35 residents. All of them are connected one way or another with the sheep farm that Robin Lee and his brother have. As sheep outfits go, this one is not small either; in fact, at about 200,000 acres and 42,000 sheep, it's the third largest here, where wool is *the* industry. But it's nothing to get a big head about—Robin came to pick us up and help wrestle our bags himself. The lodge was his idea, he said, so he tends to it and his brother concentrates on the farm.

We swayed down the track in low gear to Port Howard, clustered in a hollow between knolls. An estuary laps up against the settlement. The few barns and homes are sturdily built, mostly white and topped with pastel metal roofs. The grass and the gorse hedges are vibrantly green. Rain earlier in the day made the tidy buildings gleam in the weak sunlight. Even the mud ruts and the churned ground of a barnyard looked rich and fresh. When the Land-Rover stopped, the only sound came from off-duty sheepdogs scrabbling against their kennels to get a better look at the newcomers. After the comparative bustle of Stanley, Port Howard, out in the camp, as they say, seemed the most bucolic and peaceful habitation on earth.

At dawn the next day I was back on the knoll. I wanted to watch daylight spread over this landscape. The fresh sea wind tugged at my cap and there were dramatic clouds, with holes through which the sun began to spill. The grassland came alive in gleaming greens and browns. It could almost have been the Hebrides, or Connemara. The tide was up in the estuary, dull silver in the new light. In the spell of this peaceful scene, I hardly registered two shapes that appeared in the air at the shoulder of the headland before me. Fighter jets. Suddenly they were on me and I came awake in time to recognize the long, bulky, droop-nosed shape of Phantoms. A hundred feet off the water, they were 50 feet below me, eerily quiet and so close that the pilots and their bombardier navigators were visible people. In the next heartbeat they were gone, flashing up into the hills, but the cone of thunder they drag behind nearly knocked me down. Then it was gone away too, following the jets on their dawn patrol. For them, the Argentine mainland is only 24 minutes away.

This wasn't always the most peaceful place on earth. In the night before April 2, 1982, an Argentine assault force on practice maneuvers suddenly changed course and steamed into Port Stanley. They wrested control of the Falklands away from a token British unit. When the sun came up, the Argentines, already cold and hungry, found out where they'd been sent. Buenos Aires announced that the Malvinas had been restored to their rightful—by propinquity, if not by culture—owners.

Two weeks later a lone British Vulcan swept in under the clouds to cut the runway at Stanley airport, then, fuel-starved, went home to RAF Ascension, nearly 4,000 miles back. Royal Marines retook the old whaling station on South Georgia, 900 miles away, and the British counteroffensive in

A typical sea-trout from the Chartres River, West Falkland, where a milk can full of English brown trout were dumped in 1954.

the South Atlantic began.

Sleepy Port Howard was occupied by a thousand Argentine troops, who set up defenses around the estuary. They were eventually dislodged by units of the Special Air Service, under cover of a naval bombardment (which, ironically, caused the only real damage locally). The long, low building beyond Robin Lee's lodge is the Port Howard Social Club. One room has been made into a museum of the Battle for the Falklands—the conflict, as it is known here. Two rusty fieldpieces sit outside, and inside are memorabilia: small arms, maps, news clippings, and even a couple of ejection seats and the kit of the pilots who bailed out in them. Robin showed us the aircraft wreckage shot down over the farm; there are eight on his land in all—seven Argentine and one British, which pretty much sums up how the conflict went. It was over by June 15. Although the invaders surrendered,

Argentina has not renounced its claim to the islands; hence the British military presence.

Today, over in Tierra del Fuego, where sea-trout fishermen also go to worship, there are road signs that still insist *"Las Malvinas son Argentinas!"* Margaret Thatcher and every Falklander disagree, strongly. This is one of those places where even those who have never been off the islands refer to the United Kingdom as "home."

Robin Lee took us into what Alaskans would call the bush and Aussies the outback. This meant pointing the Rover uphill from the lodge and following the ruts from gate to gate through the sheep fence. We were off for the Warrah River.

Almost immediately we were in a high, wide and empty land. Robin drove slowly into a vast bowl rimmed by hills and carpeted in short yellow-green grass. His farm extends to the horizon in every direction. Sheep scattered from the vehicle. Even more common are small flocks of wild upland geese, and they were less shy than the domestic animals. The wind is always up, but in the sun the air was a comfortable 50 degrees. Falklanders say they get all four seasons every day, and visitors should be prepared, but neither the climate nor the terrain is nearly as forbidding as its reputation leads one to expect. These "Malvinas" are greener, gentler, less hostile than neighboring Tierra del Fuego—quite beautiful, in fact.

Soon we intersected the Green Hills Stream. There was a disturbance in the shallows—fins and tails breaking the surface. Peering over the bank revealed a lone pair of sea-trout that had come to spawn. The hen was thrashing, excavating a shallow pan in the clean river-gravel where she would spill her eggs. The male, with no competitors around to chase off, didn't quite know what to do and got in her way a lot. We didn't want to disturb spawners.

Downstream, Robin calmly nosed the Rover over the bank and dropped us into the river, where we motored majestically along, pushing up a small bow wave. ("We brake for fish.") He turned for a spot on the other shore and with no more effort than a horse getting to its feet the car heaved itself up and out of the stream. The Green Hills meets the Warrah, equally clear and clean, which flows away through the grass towards the hills at the sea. There it pinches down into a series of rocky pools that the sea-trout must negotiate on their annual run, and there we encountered the only other visitor. Andrew Tabor, a young army captain, showed us a handsome brace of trout, about 3 pounds apiece, that he'd taken on a pink krill fly after a hands-and-knees stalk of one of these tidal pockets. Even in the Falklands, sea-trout seem to be wary creatures.

We had to find the fish soon, for later we were going to Pebble Island, a bird sanctuary on the northwest edge of the archipelago. We crammed everything and everyone into the Rover and Robin motored us cross-island for hours. In midday, under a lowering sky, we crested a hill and stopped in what looked a lot like the very middle of absolutely nowhere. A wire fence ran toward us from one horizon and disappeared behind us to the other horizon. Then, crawling in from the west, came a pair of red Rovers—Pat and Bill Luxton rendezvousing to haul us the rest of the way over West Falkland to Chartres. In the Chartres River, where sea-trout began in the islands, we found them. There was certainly nothing wary about them.

In a near-gale and cold needle rain we fanned out along an elbow of the Chartres and went to work with 9- or 9 1/2-foot rods and eight-weight lines. We found sea-trout nearly everywhere, in

numbers I've never experienced before. During those three hours, the five of us brought to hand between 50 and 75 trout, and couldn't hold that many more. For periods of 30 minutes or more, on certain sections, every cast brought a strike. No wading; this was from the ledgy banks, casting into straight, narrow runs right at our feet. I began to get a bit punchy, feeling the way I have on certain Alaskan streams when the rainbows come too fast—picking line up and slapping it down, flinging the fly hard into the grassy verge on the far side and jigging it out into the current. Step-slap-tug, step-slap-tug. Kind of fun, actually. When you move fast and don't strip or shoot line, you get bi-gawd accurate. We fished bright streamers with single or double hooks. They would have pleased a steelhead—sparse hair wings, solid or ribbed Mylar bodies, green or blue or black. Best was something with at least a touch of orange, maybe to mimic the krill that fuels the Falklands food chain. Earlier, with little to lose and everything to gain, we'd experimented with dry flies and picked off the odd fish. Maybe dries would have worked here too, but I was too busy to try.

The Falklands record is a 20-pound, 2-ounce trout taken in 1986 from the Malo River, on East Falkland, which is the private water of the F.I. Fishing Club. The Malo has given up many fish well over 10 pounds. Is that because it holds a superior strain of trout—or because it is fished more and maybe better than any other Falklands river? Our trout were coloring up for the spawn, but still hot as cherry bombs. In a day and a half of sometimes-furious fishing on the Chartres, the largest sea-trout any of us took weighed 7 1/2 pounds. Half the fish we landed were under 3 pounds, and almost all the rest were under 5 pounds. Størk Halstensen, the Norwegian, and I each stuck fish that looked like 10 pounds, but lost them.

Being tired, wet, cold, and hungry is not bothersome when the fishing is fast. And it's not bothersome when you know that warm, dry clothing, a hot shower, a bottle of Scotland's finest, and a square meal awaits. With the light fading and Bill at the wheel, we slithered through mudholes and jounced across ridges back to Chartres, population 12, and Luxtons' lodge.

Next day, after fishing through the morning, we would climb back aboard the air-service Islander and fly, low and slow, out over the coast in the first really sunny weather of the trip. Below us, the beds of thick kelp waving in the surf would look like fabulous sea snakes, priming us for the penguins and seals and hosts of birds we hoped to see on Pebble Island. Beyond that lay the ordeal of the flight home, retracing the long steps across the Southern Ocean, Africa, the Atlantic, England, and the Atlantic again. But homeward-bound is a sprint with a great reward at the end, and in the meantime I was in one of earth's remotest and loveliest spots, one that I will be forever thankful to have seen.

Going Home: The British Isles

IT IS A MEASURE of the power of tradition that trout and salmon fishermen of the world still regard England as the spiritual home of their game. Whether they speak English, Spanish, Dutch, Hindu, Afrikaans, French, German, or Italian, England is for them the birthplace, where it all began. Though today the United Kingdom has been supplanted by New Zealand, Canada or the United States as the place where most of the world's coldwater fishermen would plan their dream trip of a lifetime, no other country can claim such a centuries-long and sophisticated tradition of angling literature and fine tackle. And in fact those fortunate and committed fishermen who do manage to take steelhead in British Columbia, Atlantic salmon in Quebec, rainbows in Alaska, cutthroat trout in Wyoming, landlocks in Maine, sea-trout in Argentina . . . when all those notches have been cut into their rod grips, they realize there is a final pilgrimage without which they cannot call themselves whole. It becomes time to "go home" and trace the web of their sport back to its beginnings, and to fish the brown-trout streams of England's West Country, stalk the sea-trout of Wales at night, learn the ritual of casting to the salmon of Ireland and Scotland. And perhaps visit Winchester Cathedral, to stand before the tomb of Izaak Walton and admire the stained-glass window that commemorates him. In other lands, only St. Peter and the fishers of men receive such veneration.

Such a pilgrimage can be an illuminating experience, rich in heritage and poor in the sort of angling that is nearly taken for granted in places where people and wild fish exist in more equal balance. Consider that brown trout were seeded in the Falkland Islands in the 1950s—while in Britain, where Loch Leven browns are the native species, the fishing hut Charles Cotton built for Izaak Walton almost 300 years earlier still stands on a quiet bend of the River Dove, in Dovedale. The legendary Dame Juliana Berners published her "Treatyse of Fysshnge wyth an Angle," a chapter of *The*

Boke of St. Albans that for centuries was the oldest known work on fishing, in England in 1496. And in England is the oldest active fishing club in the world, the Ellem, which has been bringing its members to order since 1831.

However, England today has some 50 million people—the populations of New York, Massachusetts *and* California—squeezed into a territory the size of Alabama. The pressure on all her natural resources, water and open land chief among them, is phenomenal. Furthermore, England is an island surrounded by the sea; no fresh water flows into the country from anywhere else. Yet the angling heritage is stronger than ever, and all those millions of "recreationists" need places to fish, and fish to catch—in a country that still permits private ownership of streams and lakes. Today rainbow and brook trout introduced from America are popular, and hatcheries keep trout fishing alive for the masses. That England has developed the most non-natural put-and-take artificial trout fisheries on earth might be viewed as a tribute to resourcefulness, not proof of "bad management."

In 1987 the seventh World Fly Fishing Championship was held near Northampton, Hampshire, in central England. Fishermen from 20 other countries got a first-hand look at what one American observer dubbed the "turkey farm" school of trout management. One of the venues was the Grafham Water, a manmade reservoir filled with water pumped *up* into it from the Ouse River, and then heavily planted with fish. (To try to find them, some competitors walked the shoreline looking for the tire marks of the stocking trucks.) There were trout in abundance, but catching them and killing them and putting them in bags for weighing began to seem peculiarly cheerless even to some of the local anglers, to whom this was normal fishing. The competition eventually moved on to flowing water, the Kimbridge stretch of the Test, one of England's most famous trout streams, but even here wild-trout devotées were disappointed.

The Test and the nearby Itchen are spring-fed, clear and lovely, with heavy insect hatches and bountiful crops of freshwater shrimp and snails for the trout to grow fat on. At first glance these placid chalkstreams are comparable to an American Henry's Fork or Yellow Breeches, but in fact they are managed to a fare-thee-well. Vegetation both in the water and on the banks is carefully pruned. Fishing is flies only. Many of the brown and rainbow trout, which often reach a respectable 3 pounds or more, are stocked. And these fish must be killed; the rules say they must not be released back into the water. Rules? Like virtually all British trout streams, these are private waters, controlled by fishing clubs, individuals, and corporations. Entry is limited and expensive. Very, very few British anglers ever get to fish their own most famous rivers.

TO MANY AMERICAN trout anglers the waters of Devon, the English West Country, are the most homelike. Devonshire is (with Cornwall) the southwestern extremity of England, that large peninsula between the English Channel and the Celtic Sea. It is relatively wild country, hilly, rural, and less populated than the rest of southern England, and much of it is windswept moorland. (Bleak and forbidding Dartmoor, where Sherlock Holmes encountered the terror of the Hound of the Baskervilles, is in Devon.)

The landscape is cut and drained by spate rivers, which are fed by runoff instead of by the constant pumping of underground springs, and so their level and appearance vary according to the

A pair of brown trout from Foston, in East Yorkshire, photographed by Arthur Oglesby.

A fat stillwater brown from one of England's many reservoir fisheries. Darrel Martin photograph.

weather. They are often narrow and crooked, flowing through unkempt brush and between sheer and undercut banks, and their bottoms range from gentle gravel to steeply shelving slate. Some, like the Wolf and the Carey, look so untouched that Anne Voss-Bark, of the Arundell Arms, often says she steps into them with the feeling that no one has ever been there before. She is a well-known fly fisherman, and the hotel she owns with Conrad, her husband, is the hub of local angling.

The stream trout here are browns, with a few grayling mixed in, and releasing them alive is allowed and even encouraged. They are small and agile, wary but aggressive, and so vividly colored even a casual fisherman senses a difference about them. These are no easy-going, pellet-fed, hatchery artifacts; they are true native trout, shaped by hundreds of generations of survival in these demanding waters. They are quick as lightning, as fast as the brown trout of the Madison and other

A brown trout from the River Itchen, one of the United Kingdom's best and most expensive private trout streams. Photograph by Darrel Martin.

fast-flowing Rocky Mountain rivers. British riverkeepers advise visiting fishermen to recite "God save the Queen" before setting the hook when a chalkstream trout rises to their fly; but down in wild Devon the little brownies are gone by "God save . . . ."

Several Devon rivers, the Tamar and the Lyd among them, are big enough to attract dependable runs of sea-trout and Atlantic salmon up to about 10 pounds. The next peninsula north of Devon and Cornwall is Wales, where jewel-like wild browns are also found. But Wales has an even better reputation for big sea-trout. They are shy fish, and most people fish for them at night, moving around in the dusk to locate a run of fish, then staying with them well past midnight.

Salmon and sea-trout historically have spawned in rivers all around the the British Isles, in numbers that seem beyond belief today. In Cromwell's time there was a "statute that commands all mas-

Another Itchen trout, this one a recently planted hatchery rainbow. The handmade split-bamboo fly rod is as de rigeur as the double-barreled shotgun on a drive-bird shoot. Darrel Martin photograph.

ters not to compel any servant or apprentice to feed upon Salmon more than thrice a week." And a thousand years before that, officers of the Roman garrison in Britain wrote of *Salar*, the silver leaper that was so common in the rivers. Difficult as it may be to envision now, even the Thames hosted a tremendous salmon run. The Industrial Revolution put an end to that, but modern cleanup efforts are paying off and a few salmon are reportedly once again moving through London to spawn far up-stream. (Anyone who has watched fishermen playing large salmon from the ancient canal walls of downtown Stockholm can imagine the possibilities for London.)

SCOTLAND has first-rate brown, brook, and rainbow trout fishing in her streams and especially her lochs, but mention the name and fishermen automatically think of salmon—"Scottish salmon"

A native brown trout, probably a wild fish, released back into the River Wye, a limestone stream in Derbyshire. Mike Weaver photograph.

symbolizing quality, like "German cars" or "French wines." Non-fishing gourmets perhaps assume Scottish salmon are a special species found nowhere else, but of course they are "merely" Atlantic salmon, the same fish that come inshore to spawn all around the perimeter of the northern Atlantic Ocean, from New England to Spain. The salmon of Scotland, however, enjoyed a royal boost to their reputation that has stuck for centuries, even though for a generation or more salmon fishing in Scotland has been deteriorating because of disease and little scientific management.

In 1966 a mysterious and deadly plague called UDN, Ulcerative Dermal Necrosis, began to devastate British and Scottish salmon when they entered their rivers. And at about the same time commercial fishing boats from Denmark, having found rich new grounds off of Greenland, began to harvest the salmon stocks at sea. (Where salmon went when they left their natal rivers had always been a mystery.) Many rivers never recovered from this double-barrelled attack, although UDN was wiped out some years ago, and treaties and fisheries protection zones (and the spread of salmon aquaculture) have limited the high-seas kill.

For centuries British aristocrats have maintained large estates in Scotland, where they went to shoot grouse and stag and cast to the great fish that migrated from the Atlantic to spawn in the clean rivers of the northern Isles. Many of the classic featherwing fly patterns that collectors revere today originated in Scotland, and to a lesser extent in Ireland and Wales, tied in the off season by the ghillies and their families to sell to the lords and ladies when they began to arrive the following spring. Guiding and fly-tying, along with farming and some salmon poaching, was an important part of their subsistence, and they sought to outdo each other with outlandishly feathered, colored, and crafted flies. (Every maker of fishing lures soon learns that the product has to catch fishermen as well as fish. And adorning some of their beautiful inventions with names such as "Lady Amherst" and "Sir Richard Sutton" probably didn't hurt sales a bit, at least to certain families.)

The upper-class cachet that still attaches to Scottish salmon fishing today attracts business types from London and the rest of the world, such as golfers who must play St. Andrews in order to round out their social portfolios. Some of the large estates are still private, maintained by their owners for the enjoyment of themselves and their friends, but more and more must open to the paying public in order to meet expenses (and the onerous British tax system). Ironically, this salmon-for-cash system may turn out to be the fish's salvation from poaching and commercial netting. The actual cash value of a rod-caught salmon—that is, the amount of money injected into the region by the sport-fisherman—far exceeds that of a netted or poached fish, and it is only a matter of time before "money talks." (As it has in the Canadian Maritimes, Norway, and Iceland, the other prime salmon fishing grounds.)

Scottish salmon rivers run to short, punchy names like Dee and Spey and Tay, and the names have stuck to types of fly dressings or lures, special tackle, or even methods of casting used there. The Tay is the largest river in Scotland. It flows through the rugged heart of the country for about 120 miles, and has 10 lochs and a dozen important tributaries. In 1922 the British rod-and-line record salmon came out of the Tay, a 64-pound submarine that may never be beaten, at least in the foreseeable future. As most British rivers, the Tay has two major runs of salmon (three, if we count the midsummer rush of grilse), the spring and the fall fish, and the waterway is divided into controlled beats that are sold or leased to anglers. There is a lot of money at stake.

There is also money, and family pride and lifestyle, tied up in the extensive small netting operations that crowd the Firth of Tay, the estuary at the river's mouth. And there is much more money in the huge hydroelectric generating system in the upper river that destroyed much prime salmon nesting and nursery areas. Finally, there's the conservation ethic, or lack of one. Poaching has reportedly died down; as the locals wryly put it, "poachers go where there are salmon." However, even the anglers themselves are partly to blame for the Scottish salmon's predicament. Catch-and-release, so strong in America and Canada, is just beginning to catch on in the British Isles. Especially among the gentry whose families have been taking salmon from the rivers for generations, there is a feeling that *we own these fish and we'll by-Harry kill them.* And most of the fishermen who lease beats for a

A colorless 18-inch put-and-take rainbow trout "harvested" from Watercress Farm, a two-acre fishing pond in Devon. Photograph by Mike Weaver.

few days at a time want to return home with a locker full of smoked fillets to show for their expense.

In a land where rivers and their fish have always been regarded as private property, government has not been inclined to get involved in the sort of comprehensive regulations that benefit fishing in the United States and a few other countries. The owner of the river, often managing his fish as a cash crop, would set his own rules. This worked fairly well when sportfishing was entirely the province of the wealthy and fish stocks were more in balance with human needs. But the increase in population, commercial development, leisure time, acid rain and other pollution, and the democratization of British society have conspired heavily against the Atlantic salmon and against wild trout. There are places, however, where the "good old days" seem to linger on. One of the best is in . . .

A Devonshire brown trout of 13 inches that came from hotel water on the Torridge River, a freestone stream where browns are stocked only at the beginning of each season. Mike Weaver photograph.

IRELAND

BALLYNAHINCH CASTLE—As a nation of anglophiles, Americans are suckers for the images that words such as "castle" call up, such as, titles and towers, spotless Rolls-Royces and muddy Land-Rovers, setter dogs, salmon beats, two-handed rods and two-barrelled shotguns. All this set on ancient estates whose echoing hallways are lined with ancestor paintings, armor, regimental standards, maybe even the yellowing silk scarf that dressed the throat of dapper Uncle Reggie when he took to the skies in his Spitfire. Tradition, in a single word—stultifying to some, reassuring to others, but with the promise that what is here has been tested and found worthy.

Some version of all this certainly flashed through our minds when my wife and I were invited to join our old friends Tom and Dawn Dorsey—he's the rod-making half of the management at

Thomas & Thomas, rod builders extraordinaire—for a week's sport with the salmon and sea-trout of Ballynahinch Castle Hotel, in Connemara, County Galway, Eire. Now my wife fishes creditably, but she has no desire to spend her precious vacation time in Labrador or Alaska, swaddled in goose down and waxed cotton in the company of a dozen strangers who speak only angling. But a real, live Irish castle is another, ahem, kettle of fish entirely. And so we accepted the invitation with unseemly haste.

But how does one dress in a castle, even one with "hotel" now part of its name? Normally I pride myself on being able to fish and travel for weeks out of a single large duffel. But that doesn't work when the destination is a place where one dresses for dinner and where rock stars and ex-presidents go to unwind. We resolved the what-shall-I-wear problem, but Napoleon when he invaded Russia probably brought less baggage.

Napoleon, it turns out, could have licked his wounds at Ballynahinch afterward, had he known the Martin family, for by then they had already owned Ballynahinch for a couple of centuries. Nor was it new then, for the Martins got it from the original landlords, the "ferocious O'Flahertys." There has been a stronghold on the site for nearly 700 years, although the present stonework is relatively recent, as it dates from only the 18th century.

Ballynahinch is, as they say, steeped in history. The most famous resident was Grace O'Malley, who made her mark as the Pirate Queen of Connaught. She moved into the castle by marrying an O'Flaherty in about 1546, when she was 16, and after he died she took over and proved herself a better man than he had been. Anything that's been around so long has seen a lot of living, and we read local histories eagerly for tales of Viking raiders, Cromwellian Roundheads, wreckers, papists, royalists, highwaymen, bluebeards, blackguards, and other ancient scoundrels. Today there is some talk about the ghost of one Owen O'Flaherty, the lord who died in a particularly unpleasant manner in the castle in 1586, but the only unearthly sounds visitors hear invariably emanate from the castle's public tap room in the wee hours.

From the salmon and sea-trout fisherman's viewpoint, the most significant owner of the place was His Highness the Maharajah Jam Sahib of Nawanagar, better known throughout the Commonwealth as Ranji the Cricketeer. (Having grown up in the era of the Raj, he apparently became more British than the British, and his nickname stems from a cricket career so ardent that some of his world records stand to this day.) A fabulously wealthy sportsman with palaces and property in England and India, he bought the large Ballynahinch estate for its fishing and shooting in 1924. It was he who caused the stone piers, fishing huts, and walkways along the castle's two and a half miles of private water to be built. Each jetty was cunningly situated, with the advice of local ghillies, so as to offer the best casting positions to cover every prime salmon and sea-trout lie in each beat. It is possible to fish much of the river in black tie and tails, should one be so inclined, and the lush landscaping and mountain backdrops complete the picture. There is, of course, a Ranji's Rock, a favored spot where the old boy killed many a salmon.

Throughout the castle are grainy photographs of Ranji—Ranji with fish, with cricket people, with family members; Ranji in Indian dress, in Western dress, and with the locals. He died of an asthma attack in 1934. The people of Ballynahinch refused to believe it at first, for the news arrived on

An American-ancestry brook trout taken in 1977 from Trenchford Reservoir in Devon's Dartmoor National Park. The fish is a mere ghost of its forebears; brook trout did not do well there, and stocking was discontinued. Photograph by Mike Weaver.

April 1 and they regarded it as something of a sick joke. The mourning that ensued was prolonged and genuine, for Ranji was truly appreciated in impoverished Connemara. Older residents still speak warmly of how he provided employment and supported local establishments and threw staff parties that turned into memorable drunks. He had a way with gifts, too—they say every fall he gave away the new cars he'd bought in Galway.

On the July day that we arrived, the sodden Irish sky cleared dramatically. The clouds blew away, the sun came out, and every morning for seven days the breakfast staff appeared in successively brighter shades of sunburn. The sons and daughters of Galway aren't accustomed to such weather. Neither, it seems, are their salmon, for although we saw many we each got but one strike that week, and they were all short, born of curiosity or boredom rather than spawning aggression. Even the

A tiny, truly wild brown trout from Dartmoor's River Teign, photographed by Mike Weaver. The Teign is an acidic moorland stream, where fish typically grow very slowly. This fish is only 8 inches long and still shows traces of its parr markings, but it is a mature adult.

prawn fishermen couldn't score. The sole salmon I saw taken was a 10-pounder, by a dignified English barrister who was accompanied by his wife and two twentyish daughters. (Each day we'd spot the girls streamside, dressed in wellies and thornproofs and corduroys, fishing hard and looking pretty rustic, and each evening they'd show up in the dining room togged out like out of the pages of Vogue.)

Everyone caught sea-trout, however, especially smaller ones that took advantage of the warm weather and low water to rise willingly to dry flies. One of the reasons the Ballynahinch fishery is unusual is because good sea-trout fishing takes place in daylight hours, not just at night, as is more common in the United Kingdom. They are handsome fish, with black backs and coin-silver bright sides decorated in black speckles, and they strike and fight hard. About 1 pound was our average,

(above) A bright, 9-pound Atlantic salmon taken in the River Teign, which also has a run of sea-trout. Note the spoon in its mouth; in North America, Atlantic salmon may be caught on flies only. Mike Weaver photograph.

(right) A visitor takes a small sea-trout on the Ballynahinch water in Connemara.

but occasionally the river gives up a 3- or 4-pounder. One chooses between fishing salmon tackle and overpowering the trout, or fishing appropriate trout tackle and risking an encounter with a salmon. The salmon are on the small side, mostly grilse in midsummer, and they normally take small, sparsely dressed flies that the trout are also fond of.

Ballynahinch as a fishing dream-spot is famous among European anglers, and has been extolled in song, story or slide lecture for 150 years. That the fisheries, trout and salmon both, apparently not only survive but prosper, speaks well of the castle's management. The castle owns two and a half miles of running water, plus lower Ballynahinch Lake; there are another 25 miles of lake and river upstream. There is no industrial or commercial development as we know it nearby whatsoever.

Ballynahinch is partly a classic British-style private-water situation, with hired ghillies and a pro-

fessional fishing manager, colorful Michael Conneely, to shoo hoi polloi away and enforce the rules, but it is set on a freestone river that would be the pride of any fishing lodge in the world. Both game species here are anadromous, and totally wild; there is no put-and-take "harvest" at Bally-nahinch. The fishing rules are as follows: Between 10 a.m. and 5 p.m., fly-fishing only; prawns (whole pink shrimp lashed to heavy hooks, a popular European salmon lure) and worms may be fished between 5 p.m. and 7 p.m. only by guests who did not take a fish on a fly earlier that day; and spinning tackle may only be used in high water and with the permission of Mr. Conneely. Fish are normally killed, but there is a limit of two fish per beat during the evening bait-fishing hours. Angling begins in the morning at 10 o'clock; beats are reassigned daily and change hands every evening at 7 o'clock. The late starting hour ensures that all guests—perhaps half or one-third are not sportsmen—may sleep undisturbed. (You may be sure that if history showed dawn to be an unusually productive fishing hour on the Ballynahinch water, the regulations would reflect that. There is normally little reason to get out at the crack, but there is a way to beat the rule—anyone fishing before 10 a.m. has been out all night.)

As is my wont, I got up each day before 7 a.m. and ensconced myself in a sunny corner of the formal dining room with a notebook and a pot of coffee. Most mornings a solid hour passed before anyone else straggled in, and I learned eventually that my behavior, especially the cryptic nonstop scribbling, caused some consternation among the staff. They were exceedingly courteous and friendly nonetheless, especially when they learned of our connection with Boston, every Irishman's home away from the auld sod. Finally, with all hands on deck and with a huge country breakfast under our belts, we would waddle off to our hired Toyota and our patient ghillies for the day's sport. The 10 a.m. deadline was never in jeopardy.

Our typical day proceeded as follows: Kit and I, under the tutelage of Sean King, and Dawn and Tom with ghillie Michael, the transplanted Dutchman, would then flog our respective beats for three hours or so, chatting, landing the odd trout, exclaiming over every salmon that showed (there were many), casting, sunning, changing flies and tactics, photographing, and walking. Altogether a pleasant warmup for the exercise to follow, namely luncheon. Lunch was in the tap room of the castle, a comfortable, dark-paneled hideout whose occupants ranged from weather-battered, gin-pickled countrymen to ageless Continental ladies exuding whiffs of Chanel. While the solid fare—patés, local salmon, chowders, thick sandwiches—was excellent, it was the drink that left a mark. It likely doesn't need repeating, but the Guinness, Heinecken and Smithwick's ("Smiddick's") on tap in an Irish pub bears little resemblance to the pitiable liquids that have been pasteurized, homoge-nized, bottled, inspected, detected, rejected, folded, spindled, and mutilated for export to our shores. A pint of Guinness, the nation's pride, is nearly a meal unto itself—a thick, chewy, almost black ale, smooth as eggnog, with but a hint of bitter and a head creamy as a dairy product. This head rises so unhurriedly that it takes minutes for the barkeep to pour a Guinness, and to me this became an allegory for Ireland. Things happen slowly, and they are worth the wait.

After such a repast, with the fishing slow and the day bright, we would opt for touring. Sitting in the back room, watching the telly over their sandwiches, our ghillies received the news bravely. We offered them our beats, and as we motored off the estate we sometimes saw them trudging happily

An evening's catch of Irish sea-trout on their way to the hotel kitchen.

The author with his trophy Atlantic salmon from the Ballynahinch water.

(far right) The maître d'hotel of Bally-nahinch Castle takes charge of a 10-pound salmon destined for the lucky angler's table.

toward the water with our rods over their shoulders.

The terror of driving on the left is exacerbated by Irish country roads, which often seem barely one car wide and are hemmed in by stone walls and thick hedges. Over these roads, in blithe disregard for order, roam trucks, tour buses, bicyclists, hikers, small local cars, large foreign cars, mopeds, motorcycles, tractors, ponies, cattle, and sheep. The net effect of all this is that one drives for what seems half a day, yet is never more than about 30 miles from Ballynahinch. There are several loops that connect rocky coastal villages—Roundstone, Clifden, Ballyconneely, Cleggan, Letterfrack—as well as landmarks such as Kylemore Abbey. In bluebird weather the scenery is breathtaking, rich with green and brown. In cold rain and a sharp wind, the granite headlands and boney vest-pocket pastures might seem forbiddingly bleak, but the tiny stone cottages, with pungent turf fires smoldering on their hearths, look snug and warm.

Upon arrival back at the castle in late afternoon, duty, honor, and curiosity demanded another go at the fishing. We swapped beats and poked and pried at the water for a couple more hours—fruitlessly, but not unhappily. Then preparations began for the long ritual of dinner—a nap, shower, dressing, and slow migration toward the tap room. There one exclaimed over the day's trout, laid out walleyed and wrinkled on the sideboard where the scales and game books are kept, and sipped drinks and chatted amiably with old and new friends. Eventually John or Moira O'Connor, the young hotel managers, appeared to inquire about one's day and to hand out the evening's menu.

Dinners were, to sum up, lovely; many courses, served with linen and silver, in a distinctive and appealing cuisine. The high-ceilinged dining room, candlelight gleaming on its polished wood floor and antique furnishings, hummed with quiet conversation. The lips of vintage bottles clinked against crystal goblets. A log fire crackled in the ornate green marble fireplace. Moonlight silvered the lower pools of Beat #1, at the foot of the terrace just through the tall French doors. There were rich desserts and Cuban cigars for the truly hedonistic. As midnight approached, music and song began to drift out of the tap room as a visiting pipe band or local minstrels went at it.

Did we not fish at night? Yes, once. As dusk fell, slowly in these high latitudes, the trout became increasingly active, rising loudly all around. The nightly gnats became active too, unfortunately—insidious little horrors that made their way past cuffs and bandannas and turtlenecks to latch onto flesh. They seemed to thrive on bug repellent. As it is impossible to strip line and swat at the same time, we gave it up and retreated to the bar. More dedicated fishermen, some with headnets, stayed out late and often, and scored big on small sea-trout.

Scandinavia

AN OBSERVER armed only with the knowledge that trout and salmon prefer cold, clean water could spin a globe and guess with little hesitation that Scandinavia might be an ideal region for those great gamefish. From Finland in the east to Iceland (in fact, all the way to Greenland, which officially is part of Denmark and which has large, and largely inaccessible, populations of arctic charr and some Atlantic salmon) on the west, the entire land area lies above latitude 55 degrees north and much of it extends up beyond the Arctic Circle—very nearly *too* cold for salmonids.

As it happens, of course, much of Scandinavia is blessed with first-rate native populations of sea-trout (migratory browns), brown trout, arctic charr, and Atlantic salmon. For salmon angling, the best waters of Norway and Iceland have, for generations, been the near-private preserves of wealthy European (particularly British) families and business cartels who lease the rivers from their native owners for their own sport. The most expensive fishing on earth today is probably those salmon pools on the River—in Norway, which in 1989 were offered to sportsmen for the price of $15,000 per rod per week.

ICELAND: *Alone With its Salmon*

FROM THE SALMON fisherman's viewpoint, Iceland has everything in its favor. There are many rivers and streams and relatively few inhabitants to overfish or pollute those streams. The craggy terrain is bare and rocky, the product of thousands of years of still-active volcanism in a subarctic environment. This means there is usually plenty of room for a fly fisherman's backcast—no streamside vegetation—and the rivers stay clear even after heavy rains, because there is almost no mud to stir up. The relative scarcity of aquatic insects is not a problem because the anadromous fish do

(above) A well-marked sea-trout caught in the Laxá i Adaldal in Iceland. Photograph by R. Valentine Atkinson.

(left) Roland Holmberg, with the net, and the author show off a streamlined 24-pound Atlantic salmon from Norway's Gaula River.

most of their feeding at sea.

Despite the name of the country, its temperatures are moderated considerably by near-shore ocean currents; while it never gets downright hot, it doesn't get extremely cold either. The stark landscape is always impressive and eerily beautiful; and the Icelanders are as warm and outgoing as their own volcanic hot springs. Only the wind is the angler's enemy—the North Atlantic wind that sweeps unhindered across the treeless land.

Iceland doesn't even have any neighbor countries to share its resources with—or to protect its resources from. Iceland is, in fact, the least-densely populated European country and the most recently settled; yet its parliament, the Althing, which was established in the year 930, is Europe's oldest governing body. The first settlers were Norsemen—Vikings striking out westward from

(above) The photographer with a 27-pound male Atlantic salmon, also caught in "the big laxa" the Laxá i Adaldal, one of Iceland's top big-salmon rivers. R. Valentine Atkinson photograph.

(right) The way it was, and often still is, in Norway's élite Atlantic salmon rivers. The photographer's host washes down the day's catch from the River Vosso. Arthur Oglesby photograph.

mainland Scandinavia—who arrived barely a lifetime before that date. So little has the population of Iceland been diluted in the intervening millennium that the modern language still closely resembles Old Norse and the entire country often seems to behave like an overgrown-but-still-close family.

This sort of cultural homogeneity, the very opposite of the American melting pot, makes for a remarkable national unanimity of thought and opinion. To an American, for Icelanders to agree on such matters as environmental protection has something of the air of a household sitting amicably down to dinner to plan a course of action. The benefits to Iceland's native Atlantic salmon, brown trout, and arctic charr have been many, even in this nation of commercial fishermen. The 60 or so angling rivers on the island are perhaps the most zealously protected on earth—and among the most expensive to boot. As in Norway, the right to fish certain select salmon rivers may cost more

than $1,000 in U.S. currency a day per rod. Since Iceland became independent from Denmark in 1945, it has been illegal for a non-national to own an Icelandic river, and every year the value of this regulation becomes clearer to everyone in the country. Although relatively few anglers are involved, sportfishing is a major revenue-producer.

Iceland has never been famous as the home of large salmon; a fish of more than 20 pounds is unusual (some partisans of Norwegian or Canadian rivers dismiss Iceland as a place for grilse fishermen). However, only an exceedingly spoiled light-tackle angler would dismiss an 8- or 12-pound gamefish as "too small"—especially when most Icelandic rivers yield up season-long average catches of two to ten such salmon per day per rod, and those fish are often very strong and energetic battlers. Numbers-wise, this may seem like small potatoes compared to an above-average day in Alaska, which for perhaps two-thirds the cost can produce 40 or more rainbow trout, Dolly Varden, and Pacific salmon up to 10 pounds or more, but in the Atlantic such averages are hard to beat.

The salmon overshadow two pairs of excellent gamefish that are just as plentiful in certain Icelandic rivers, the sea-run and riverine strains of both brown trout and arctic charr. It may be stretching geographic boundaries a bit to do so, but a number of well-traveled fishermen call Iceland the best trout fishing in Europe—the browns, which may be very plentiful, average a couple of pounds and occasionally exceed 6 pounds, while an unusually large charr will be twice that size. Certain rivers favor these species, especially above waterfalls that halt the upstream migration of the salmon, so it is possible to fish for them at far less than Atlantic-salmon prices. Still, despite the river owners' and booking agents' best efforts, very few Americans travel to Iceland for anything but the glamorous salmon.

NORWAY: *Here Lie Legends*

THE MOST EXPENSIVE, demanding, and potentially the most rewarding, Atlantic salmon fishing on earth is in coastal Norway—which is nearly the entire country. And in the mountainous interior, the native brown trout and charr fishing can be superb as well. Norway is still rural, comparatively undeveloped, enjoys a top-shelf standard of living, and is largely untroubled by pollution except in the south, which is the more populated end of the country and which also suffers from acid precipitation (courtesy of industrial emissions in the United Kingdom, situated upwind).

As in the rest of Scandinavia and the British Isles, rivers are privately owned and often generate respectable incomes for their owners. A plain Norwegian farmer who drives a big BMW probably inherited a choice pool or two on a good salmon river, and charges plenty for the fishing rights. Thus many Norwegian rivers have been the exclusive turf of large corporations or titled British families for many years. (The British "invasion" of Norway began in about 1830, and present-day Norwegian sporting ethics and tackle can be traced directly to Britain.) Closed to the angling public, they have become the stuff of legends. Others, especially in far northern Norway, generate their own tales by being so big and so wild. Stories, rumors, and half-truths have circulated for decades about rivers such as the Arøy, Vosso, Alta, Laerdal, Tana, and others, involving glimpses of incredible 90-pound salmon and tales of 10-hour battles under the midnight sun that finally end when the exhausted fisherman's heart gives out. As it happens, some of these might even be true, especially the ones that

Emotions run high on Norway's expensive private waters: Angler and guide celebrate a bright Gaula River salmon. Photograph by Michael Fong.

(above) A Norwegian salmon goes to the smokehouse on a bed of streamside ferns in the trunk of an old Saab.

(right) A brace of nearly identical 33-pound salmon taken from the River Vosso by the photographer, Arthur Oglesby. Note the bait-casting tackle.

date from Victorian times, before hydroelectric dams cut off spawning grounds on some rivers and before commercial drift-netting in the fiords became so widespread.

For a taste of those legends, read Ernest Schwiebert's anthology called *Death of a Riverkeeper*. The best piece is the story of Schwiebert's 1965 visit with Count Denisoff, the mysterious Russian refugee (from the 1917 Revolution) who for more than 50 years held the fishing rights on the Arøy. The Arøy, which has since been crippled by a hydro installation, is a short, violent river that drops in a series of thunderous falls into its tidal pool. Only the strongest salmon could spawn on its cobblestone bottom, and over the decades Count Denisoff and his fortunate guests had killed many salmon greater than 50 pounds, and several in the seventies. Behind the fishing house was a junkyard of enormous two-handed rods smashed by the greathearted fish that effortlessly traversed

A Baltic sea-trout caught among the small islands of the Stockholm Archipelago.

those cataracts. Schwiebert found standing over and casting into the maelstrom from the Count's precarious walkways a little frightening and, borrowing his host's term, he called the story "The Platforms of Despair."

Today, the fisherman who absolutely must have a 45-pound Atlantic salmon for his trophy wall ends up spending many, many days and nights in Norway if he can afford it, and if he can worm his way into the old-boy network that still envelopes rivers such as the Alta. The chances of taking a fish such as that are slim indeed, but they are there. So, still, are salmon up to 15 pounds larger. (Certain élite Canadian rivers periodically yield fish of such size also, but new conservation legislation makes it more difficult to kill them; and many old-line salmon anglers still like to kill their fish. Norway has no such rules, nor are there restrictions against taking salmon on weighted flies, or even spinning tackle, spoons, or bait.)

Although fish size varies from river to river—as it does throughout the Atlantic salmon world, because fish return only to their natal rivers, thus confining and concentrating the gene pool—Norway on average probably yields larger salmon than other countries. Any fish over 20 pounds is memorable, but 30-pounders are fairly common too. And there are dozens of excellent smaller and less famous rivers that are easier to get time on and easier, and much less expensive, to fish. In 1988 the government finally banned commercial netting for salmon in the fjords. Since those nets have reportedly taken up to 80 percent of the fish returning to certain rivers, the numbers and size of the salmon passing by angler's lures can only improve.

Every salmon river and tidal pool has its share of sea-trout as well. In a region not so blessed with salmon, Norway's superb sea-trout fishery would get much more attention than it does. Nevertheless, the best fishing for trout and charr is in the myriad of high lakes and streams scattered along the mountainous border with Sweden and on the remote Finnmark plateau, where Norway meets Finland, the Soviet Union, and the Barents Sea. (Some of the largest lakes also hold a subspecies of lake trout, deep-dwelling and growing to about 20 pounds.) The rule of thumb, according to Norwegians, is that the farther north one goes in their country, and the farther from a road one hikes in, the better the fishing becomes.

SWEDEN AND FINLAND: *Inland Riches*

THE BALTIC SEA, which separates these countries, brings them both excellent Atlantic salmon and especially sea-trout fishing. The key is the Baltic's vast population of herring, which supports many small commercial netting operations and also provides a rich bounty for these gamefish to fatten upon before migrating inshore to spawn. The spring sea-trout are normally 8 to 10 pounds; in the fall, after an easy summer of herring-bashing in the brackish, temperate water of the Baltic, they may reach twice those numbers. (Salmonids they are not, but it's worth noting that the Baltic is also home to an unusual subspecies of salt-tolerant northern pike locally known as sea-pike. They too feast upon the herring, and routinely grow to more than 30 pounds; occasionally, 50-pounders have been caught.)

Atlantic salmon also make their way through the Baltic into Swedish and Finnish rivers to spawn, but these fish are generally smaller than the salmon of Norway. Even the river that flows right

A salmaa, or Finnish salmon; this one a male of about 7 pounds. A.J. McClane photograph.

through the heart of Stockholm, canaled between ancient walls of stone and arched over by dozens of bridges, still has an annual run of salmon. Ted Dalenson, a fishing outfitter who grew up in Stockholm, once told me he'd caught hundreds of salmon downtown when he was a boy—but the big ones, he said, are tough to hang on to; they run downstream to the next bridge and break off on the pilings. Outside the city, the hundreds of small, rocky islands in the western Baltic that make up the Stockholm Archipelago are a comfortable and beautiful place to fish, resembling Maine's Penobscot Bay and similarly seeming to have stepped out of time somewhat.

The two most famous sea-trout rivers of Europe are in Sweden; the River Em and the Mörrum, which are about the only waters that yield sea-run browns comparable to the huge fish of Tierra del Fuego. They host salmon too, naturally; the Mörrum has a reputation for producing the odd fish of

40 pounds or more. Fishing the spring run on the Em—for those few fortunate enough to get permits—can be notably adventurous. The spring freshet brings the river up over its wooded banks, and fishermen often have to contend not only with fast, high water but also with hot fish up to 10 pounds or more that rip line off through the trees. Much as Scandinavian fishermen revere their salmon, they say that pound for pound the sea-trout is a tougher adversary on rod and reel, answering the sting of the hook with a berserk downstream charge that can almost never be turned.

Sweden is more forested than Norway, and much less mountainous (and also more populated and developed), but here too the fishing steadily improves as one goes farther north. Swedes say their country has almost a hundred thousand ponds and lakes, and many of them hold salmonids of at least one sort, native or exotic. Among Scandinavian countries, Sweden has the most active hatchery program, which extends even to poisoning out coarse species in some southern and central lakes and replacing them with trout. The southern, more developed part of the country is now heavily stocked with American-transplant rainbows and even brook trout, in addition to relocated native browns and charr, but in the northern regions there are strong populations of wild brown trout that grow to 5 or 6 pounds, and reports of browns from the larger, deeper lakes that reach 10 kilos, or about 22 pounds. The charr populations (*Salvelinus alpinus*, the race that Linnaeus himself named in the 18th century) grow as one moves northward too, and these are popular with ice fishermen.

Across the way, in Finland, the chief difference is the language, which is about as different from Swedish or Norwegian as it is from English. If anything, Finland is dotted with even more lakes and threaded with more rivers (and home to more and thicker clouds of hungrier mosquitos). Lake Inari, on the Soviet border in Finnish Lapland, gave up the country's record brown trout, a fish of a bit more than 33 pounds.

In July 1989, the ninth World Fly Fishing Championship was held in Kuusamo, in northeastern Finland just below the Arctic Circle. The main venues were the Kitka and Kuusinki rivers, which flow across the border into immense Lake Pyaozero (Paanajarvi, to the Finns) in the Soviet Union. The competing fishermen found brown trout—big ones; a French team member took a 16-pounder—moving determinedly up the rivers from the Soviet lakes to spawn. These are summer-run fish, and their young stay in the rivers for generally two and a half years before heading down to the lake to complete the maturing process. Kuusamo, the nearest big town, is a popular hunting and fishing destination for Scandinavians, so the Finnish fisheries board also stocks a number of these rivers with hatchery browns. Summer anglers find a mix of wild and planted trout that range in size from a few ounces to well over 12 pounds. The two are generally easy to distinguish. The wild spawners are much larger, at least 4 pounds or so. They also behave differently; like salmon, they don't eat while on their migration and have to be provoked somehow into striking an artificial lure. Also like Atlantic salmon (and unlike the Pacific species), these trout do not necessarily die after digging their redds and laying their eggs.

Like brown trout the world around, these Scandinavian fish are caught more readily at night, even the non-feeding migrants. But this is no hardship in the far reaches of Norway, Sweden, and Finland, for during the summer season the sun simply never sets. Fishermen who travel north far enough find themnselves in Lapland, the Arctic region that crosses political boundaries.

A Norwegian grilse, an immature Atlantic
salmon, destined for the smokehouse.

Mainland Europe

THE HOME OF WESTERN CIVILIZATION was also home to one of the world's most admired and eagerly sought-after salmonids—still the quintessential trophy trout to many fishermen, the brown, *Salmo trutta*. Native in the post-glacial era from the Black Sea in the south to the Arctic coast of Scandinavia and Siberia, it has been transplanted in its various races—sea-run, riverine, lake-dwelling—all over the world, most notably to North America, Australia, and New Zealand.

Unfortunately for the brown trout—and the rest of Europe's native salmonids, from the various huchens to Atlantic salmon, charr, and marble and other trout—western Europe is the most densely populated and heavily developed and industrialized region of its size on earth. Even in rural regions, intensive agriculture over centuries has left its marks on streams and lakes. "Salmonids" and "development" are generally antithetical, and in most of Europe (with a few shining exceptions) the coldwater fisheries are but a faint, pleasant echo of what once was, despite the introduction and widespread stocking of rainbow trout from California and (less common) brook trout from Maine. Parts of eastern Europe, for all that its people have been denied the material advances of the 20th century by Communism, are still something of a trout angler's paradise, with thousands of clean, cold waters and millions of acres of forest and mountain. They also hold some unusual salmonids that are unique to the region.

However, the future holds some mild promise for trout and salmon in western Europe. The lowering of trade and other barriers between European nations scheduled for 1992 may lead the way to a more uniform fisheries code as well, especially in countries with public waters in common. The dramatic fall of the Iron Curtain has allowed free travel between East and West, and the attendant exchange of ideas and ways of doing things may also help spread more enlightened fisheries and

A brown trout from the Pyrenees Mountains of Spain.

water-conservation practices. The Green Party, the once-radical political group dedicated to environmental concerns, has made great strides in the 1980s; "mainstream" Europeans from conservative German burghers to British aristocrats have begun to support Green planks in their various political platforms, and the environmental movement in Europe has by now perhaps outstripped North America's in its activism and demands. (Unfortunately, it has farther to go there than in the New World.) Trout and salmon will never regain their former numbers, but if air and water pollution, commercial overfishing, the construction of hydroelectric dams, and building along shorelines and wetlands can be curbed, European coldwater fisheries can only improve. The conservation movement is also growing strongly among anglers. In addition, the idea of catch-and-release is slowly catching on in Europe, and a number of wild fisheries are now protected by no-kill regulations.

This has been held up partly by the widespread notion that catch-and-release is cruel, that it is far more humane to kill a fish quickly than to play it nearly to exhaustion before handling it and releasing it, half-dead, back into the water just so the same thing may happen again. Along with the environmentalist Greens, animal-rights activists are becoming increasingly powerful in Europe (and in America). In 1988 there was a celebrated case in Germany, where a judge fined the organizers of a catch-and-release fishing competition—who no doubt felt themselves staunch conservationists—the equivalent of $700 each for promoting cruelty to animals. The verdict that fish do feel pain when dragged from the water was based upon testimony from biologists as to the increased cardiac and respiratory rates of hooked fish. Several years before, a letter published in *Plaisirs de la Pêche*, the French fly-fishing magazine, perhaps gave us a glimpse of the middle future. It suggested that anglers should fish with flies and lures that were not merely barbless but *hookless*, and that for the sake of humanity fishing should become a sport of enticing fish to the strike alone.

Just as Europeans often can't comprehend the vastness and geographical diversity of America and Canada until they see it for themselves, many Americans simply do not realize how small Europe is. America has only one or two states that can be driven completely through in the hour or so it takes to cross Switzerland, Austria, Belgium, or the Netherlands. This complicates conservation efforts considerably. Fish know nothing of political borders, but many of Europe's major watersheds span provinces or districts in several different countries, and the gamefish and water levels and quality are thus subject to that many different legal systems. What is protected here may be completely open a mile downstream. Rivers such as the Rhine, the Rhône, and the Danube drain most of Europe, and while they once were major trout and salmon breeding grounds, now they are little more than commercial highways. (Though huchen, often called Danube salmon in Europe, still reach 70 pounds or so in that river, and very large browns are still dredged periodically out of the Rhine and the Rhône.) Conservation is a matter of international cooperation.

While few fishermen from the rest of the world travel to mainland Europe specifically for trout and salmon, fishing there offers considerable rewards, though not often relating to the size and number of fish. This is "cultured" fishing, in lands that have been catering to visitors for centuries. Intimate inns, hotels, pensions, gasthaus and chateaux abound. Streams often meander through vineyards, gentle wooded valleys, or forests that resemble carefully tended arboretums. Throughout rural Europe the pace of life is slow, somehow simultaneously sophisticated and provincial; local food and wine are prepared lovingly and served proudly. There are few scars on the landscape, and there is not even a faint glimpse of the original wilderness. That is available too, however, especially in eastern Europe, where the Tatra and the Carpathian mountains, for example, are still wild and abound with wild game.

Europe still has many private and thus expensive fishing waters, or their alternative, the overcrowded public waters. One of the most popular coldwater gamefish is the grayling, and it is usually lumped in with salmonids on fishermen's hit parades. Although American trout have been widely introduced in Europe, they generally have not fared very well (with some exceptions) and so there has been a great deal of re-stocking of native fish—moving them from region to region, watershed to watershed—to increase their range and to escape pollution.

SPAIN: *Trout and Salmon Sleeper*

IT IS LITTLE KNOWN in the United States, but Spain has a coldwater fishing tradition that is almost as old and well-developed as that of Britain, embracing not only trout but also Atlantic salmon. Some of it is protected by strict no-kill regulations and fly-fishing-only. As in the United Kingdom, the very best waters are private and expensive, essentially off-limits to the locals. Nevertheless, though trout fishing is popular among Spaniards (Spain has been an ardent competitor in the World Fly Fishing Championships, which inevitably involve trout, and hosted the event in 1984), there are few visiting anglers. Along the better rivers there is even an extensive network of comfortable fishing huts, maintained by the government, and regular patrols of river *garda* to watch over the fishing. The fact that Gen. Franco was an ardent angler may have something to do with the generally good state of Spain's trout fishery; another factor is the relatively low population density and state of development in the country, which to most American tourists seems to be slumbering peacefully in about the 15th century.

Northern Spain has excellent populations of still-wild (native *and* naturally reproducing) brown trout from the eastern edge of the Pyrenees Mountains all along the north coast and down to Portugal. There are about a dozen recognized Atlantic salmon rivers that flow down along this coast, into the Atlantic Ocean's Bay of Biscay, out of the Cantabrian Mountains. (Portugal is the southern extremity of the salmon's range on the eastern side of the Atlantic; if they went any farther south they'd be in Africa, or at least the Mediterranean, and that's too warm.)

Although the latitude is the same as New England's, many of the Cantabrian peaks are snow-capped year-round, and their rivers are cold and well oxygenated and support healthy hatches of aquatic insects. There and in the Pyrenees—with their very rocky, steep, clear rivers seasonally swollen by snowmelt—is some of the best North American-style trout fishing in Europe. Lake fishing abounds also, in natural impoundments and those formed by hydroelectric dams. California rainbows were stocked decades ago, but the program was discontinued when the rainbows refused to thrive; brook trout didn't work either.

The streams and rivers of southern Spain are often diverted or drawn down for agricultural use and get too warm for salmonids; the biggest trout are always found in the deeper reservoirs or lakes. Spain's Azores Islands, 1,200 miles offshore, also have trout and salmon, but the fishing is anything but developed—or even well-known. There are said to be spectacular trout in the large volcanic lakes, remote and hard to reach.

FRANCE: *The Old World*

NATIVE WILD and stocked *fario*, or brown trout, are spread throughout France, but as in much of western Europe, the best waters are private and heavily restricted. Public trout stocks have been hit hard in this century by pollution, dams, agriculture, overfishing, and antiquated sporting ethics and regulations. However, in a more modern and democratic style, France now has many regional TOS (Truite, Ombre [grayling], Saumon) associations and two Atlantic salmon societies that campaign actively for better fisheries management, catch-and-release, and clean-up of polluted waters.

The interior of the country offers extraordinarily beautiful rural settings and peaceful streams and

A heavily spotted French rainbow from Normandy, indistinguishable from its northwestern American cousins. Photograph by Darrel Martin.

lakes. Along the Atlantic coast, Normandy has good sea-trout runs, with fish occasionally still reaching 20 pounds, and many stocked, still waters, and in Brittany the sea-trout and Atlantic salmon both are making a comeback. France's best wild trout streams—so long as they have not been dammed, diverted, or developed somehow—are in the French Alpine region and the Pyrenees Mountains, which are still quite wild on both the French and Spanish sides. The fish typically are small browns, up to 2 pounds or so, and charr.

The French are increasingly borrowing British-style stocking techniques, which have led to new stillwater trout fisheries, but coldwater conditions can vary widely around the country with more than just geography and weather. French fishing is subject to many different rules and regulations that are administered by federal, regional, and local government agencies as well as by local sports-

A Gacka River brown trout, the colors of its markings altered by the underwater light, cruises through lush vegetation in search of freshwater snails, shrimps, and insects. Michel Roggo photograph.

men's associations, syndicates and private landowners.

BELGIUM, HOLLAND AND LUXEMBOURG

ONCE THE NETHERLANDS must have been home to thousands of Atlantic salmon; this small country contains the mouth of the mighty Rhine River. Now the river, and the city of Rotterdam that grew up around it, is the commercial gateway to northern Europe. Many rivers of the Low Countries have been ruined, or at least degraded beyond the tolerance of trout and salmon, by industrial pollution and the simple pressures of ultrahigh population density. Ironically, those unmolested enough at least to appear clean and serene have often been made untenable for trout by hugely popular campsites. Unlike rushing mountain streams, which are heavily oxygenated and whose currents carry foreign matter away quickly, these calm flows and flat, meandering waterways get dirty quickly, stay that way longer, and reach higher temperatures as well.

Still, a few Atlantic salmon doggedly make their way into coastal Belgian streams. In southern Belgium the Danube salmon are gone but the now-peaceful rivers of the Ardennes Forest still hold wild brown trout, and they are also stocked with rainbows originally from California. It is difficult, demanding fishing, but salmonids have a strong local following. Neighboring Luxembourg, which shares some rivers with Belgium, was the site of the first World Fly Fishing Championship, in 1981.

SWITZERLAND AND AUSTRIA

THE MOUNTAIN streams and lakes of these small countries offer some of the best native and stocked trout fishing left in western Europe, and Austria's River Traun is such an active fishery that highly specialized tackle and techniques have evolved there—not to mention a few fishermen, such as Roman Moser, who have achieved world fame as angling innovators (always a sure sign of an active fishery). Austria's lowland rivers now support healthy populations of imported rainbows that winter over and reproduce naturally. The riverine brown trout are unusually colorful and brightly marked. The high-mountain streams of Switzerland have the typically vibrant but small brown trout of such cold, nearly sterile waters, but there are very large browns and charr in the deep lakes. The Swiss and the Austrians are among the leaders of the Green movement, and catch-and-release has become popular among anglers of both countries.

ITALY AND GERMANY

THE UNUSUAL marble trout and Lake Garda trout of Yugoslavia also appear on the west side of the Adriatic Sea (maybe we should put that another way, for Lake Garda is in Italy). In Italy marble trout are called *marmorata* and they reportedly grow up to 4 feet long—this without the "benefit" of a massive hatchery and stocking program; Italy's marmorata are all wild fish. Italy has no Atlantic salmon, but native species include brown trout and charr, and these were augmented early in the 20th century by stockings of American rainbows. The best trout waters are in the comparatively vast, mountainous, rural regions of the Alps and the Appenine Mountains, where there are thousands of streams and lakes. Central Italy, where the climate is hotter, nevertheless has good, and much less crowded, trout streams also. Germany has become something of a destination for trout fishermen from other parts of Europe, thanks to its extensive trout stocking and management programs. There are sea-trout rivers in the north, and in the Black Forest of southern Germany and in the Alpine high country the waters produce native brown trout up to some 6 pounds; rainbow trout along the upper Danube reportedly reach 10 pounds.

POLAND, CZECHOSLOVAKIA AND ROMANIA

TAKING A CUE from the British, Poland adopted fly-fishing more than a century ago, and along with it a national love of trout. One Professor Rozwadowski published a nationally famous treatise on the sport in 1899, and fly-fishing has been so popular that national competitions have been held in Poland since 1963. Northern Poland has a Baltic coastline with the expected runs of sea-trout and

A pugnacious-looking rainbow in the same section of the Gacka River, also photographed by Michel Roggo.

A Yugoslavian rainbow. Photograph by Darrel Martin.

a few Atlantic salmon, but there is an unexpected trophy there as well. Thanks to extensive stocking of rainbow trout in those coastal rivers in the 1970s, there are now locally strong runs of steelhead. Inland, along with freestone streams there are a number of clean lakes, and viable aquatic-insect populations throughout to support trout. To supplement the rainbows and the native browns, Poland's aggressive hatchery system introduced brook trout as well.

As befits a Communist (at least until very recently) country, especially one that espouses fly-fishing, all its waters are open to anyone, with the result that stocked fish are very soon caught out. Southern Poland reportedly has more fish than the north, but they are smaller. The more developed south also has more pollution, and those rainbows that arrived in the 1970s did not settle in well, though a reservoir stocking program seems to be changing that. Huchen are said to occur in only

two of Poland's rivers, the Dunajec and one of its tributaries, the Poprad, and reports are they had to be stocked there.

Czechoslovakia, like Poland, has its best trout populations in the wild spate streams of the high Tatra Mountains along their mutual border. And in Rumania trout fishing is very popular, enough so that the country regulates and manages its salmonids and its anglers well. For example, federal law stipulates that salmonids may be fished for only with artificial baits, and in freshwater with flies only. About a third of the country is high enough and cold enough for native brown trout up to 8 pounds, lake trout (European lake trout, that is; *Salmo trutta lacustris*, a stillwater brown, not the fork-tailed North American laker, which is actually a charr, *Salvelinus namaycush*) and huchen, as well as some stocked brook trout and rainbows. The high glacial lakes of the Carpathian Mountains pro-

A small but deep-bellied marble-brown trout hybrid from Yugoslavia. Darrel Martin photograph.

duce some stunningly beautiful trout, including a brook trout subspecies marked with red and orange stars. It interbreeds with browns to produce so-called tiger trout, striped and studded with black spots.

YUGOSLAVIA: *Europe's Best*

IN SPITE OF POSSIBLE claims to the contrary from Scandinavians or Englishmen, the best trout fishing in Europe is likely to be in Yugoslavia. It is a sparsely inhabited, stunningly beautiful, underdeveloped country made up of six different nations (Montenegro, Macedonia, Croatia, Serbia, Bosnia-Herzegovina, and Slovenia). More than one third of the Socialist Federal Republic of Yugoslavia is completely forested; three-quarters is mountain and plateau. Overall there are nearly 2,000 significant rivers and streams, plus a full complement of lakes—none, of course, private; seemingly all watched over by one or another angling club or fisheries research institute. They range from clear, freestone mountain rivers bounded by thick forests to meandering meadow chalkstreams. And, geologically speaking, the entire country is limestone, a morphology that favors fertile trout water. Some of the top rivers, such as the famous Gacka, in Slovenia, are so dense with food—thick and plentiful hatches of aquatic insects from tiny midges to mayflies to huge stoneflies—that they produce growth rates in trout of as much as 2 1/2 pounds per year, and trophy native browns as big as 14 pounds. The biologists who tend these waters so well are sought as speakers at fisheries conventions all around the world.

Little wonder then that expert European anglers eagerly anticipate their Yugoslavian excursions, for salmonids and also for the large and plentiful grayling. They are so taken by the charms of the country and its superb fishing that they happily abide by the strict catch-and-release rules.

Along with its highly colored native browns and the rainbows (introduced from California in 1937) that took to the country as though it were home, Yugoslavia also boasts several races of ancient salmonids, including the Lake Garda trout (*Salmo carpio*); *Salmo letnica*, the Ohrid trout, which was unsuccessfully transplanted to Minnesota in the 1930s; the softmouth trout, which looks like a brown trout with the underslung mouth of a sucker, and the marble trout, *Salmo marmoratus*. All these races are thought to be descended from a common ancestor with the brown trout. Marble trout are common and often large; they were, for example, the only salmonids in the equally famous Soca River (until browns were transplanted there just after 1900). The biggest marble trout on record include a 44-pounder taken in 1928, and a 46-pounder that came out of the Moaca River in 1968. Like huchen, marble trout prefer deep pools near fast water. There is reportedly also a small fall run of huchen—Danube salmon—in some Yugoslavian rivers, and there are charr and European lake trout in the cold lakes.

Asia

THE SOVIET UNION: *Mystery Wrapped in an Enigma*

FOR DECADES, western sportsmen have wondered about fishing for trout and salmon behind the Iron Curtain. In the Soviet Union there seemed to be plenty of possibilities for both kinds of fish—those possibilities tempered, however, by the fact that the Soviet Union has been swept by conflict and shortages of food, if not outright famine, since before the Romanovs were toppled in 1917. One school of thought had it that anything in the Soviet countryside that could run, crawl, fly or swim had long ago been hunted down and eaten by hungry peasants or by Red Army troops stationed in the forests. Others held that, although the population is now about 265 million inhabitants, they are spread out over one of the largest countries on earth—one in which there are vast regions, particularly north of the 60th parallel on the Asian side, that are still completely empty—and *some* wildlife must have survived and might even be flourishing today, despite the Soviet Union's dismal record of pollution. On top of that, the Party bosses, first among equals in the Soviet Union's "classless society" must have reserved for themselves some superb fishing and hunting on their dachas, the country estates within helicopter range of the Kremlin and the various regional capitals.

The Black Sea, the Caspian Sea, and the Aral Sea drainages all evolved their own races of brown trout. John Rayner, who was chief of wildlife research for the state of Oregon, described the Kura strain of Caspian trout as reaching 112 pounds and spawning but once in its lifetime. He also speculated that the Aral trout was in fact the same as the brown trout still found in northern Turkey. If so, the subspecies may yet survive there, for the Aral Sea has diminished by about one-third since the mid-1960s (its two major feeder rivers wholly diverted to irrigate the Soviet cotton crop) and its remaining water is too salty for fish. The Black and Caspian seas and their tributaries have been

severely dammed and polluted also.

On the far eastern end of the Soviet Union, in the rivers of the Kamchatka and Chukchi peninsulas and the land in between (and even southward into Korea), there are today rainbow trout, arctic charr, and major runs of Pacific salmon and even steelhead, the sea-run rainbow. The native people of that region are the same as Alaska's, and so are the fish and game species. In the west the Soviet Union rubs up against Scandinavia and the Baltic Sea, legendary for both trout and salmon. Surely the same fishing must exist on the Russian side of those borders, an arbitrary line that no wild creature would respect? So it proved to be—but hardly in legendary proportions.

Every year since about 1985, one or two groups of American anglers have been allowed to fish for Atlantic salmon on the Kola Peninsula, near Murmansk on the Barents Sea. To date, the results have been disappointing; very few fish. However, Atlantic salmon fishing is anything but predictable. Were the fishermen just at the wrong place at the wrong time? Because of weather and water conditions, it's easily possible to miss a run of salmon even in a flourishing fishery, especially when the fishermen have a "window" of only a week or so. Their Soviet hosts naturally assured them that has been the case. So it turned out to be, perhaps. In the fall of 1989, one of those small groups of Americans finally connected with the Kola salmon, and returned home with glowing stories of success—about 120, the largest 28 pounds, taken and released in a week's hard fishing. The news can only spur this form of United States-Soviet commerce.

And what of general trout fishing? That is more of a mystery. But we have clues. In July 1989, the ninth World Fly Fishing Championship was held in Kuusamo, in northeastern Finland just below the Arctic Circle. The main venues were the Kitka and Kuusinki rivers, which flow across the border into immense Lake Pyaozero in the Soviet Union. The competing fishermen found brown trout—big ones; a French team member took a 16-pounder—moving determinedly up the rivers from the Soviet lake to spawn in Finnish stream gravel.

(They also found a border that was pretty permeable, even months before the Iron Curtain generally collapsed into tatters late in 1989. Competitors discovered a gravel road that went through the forest into the Soviet Union, controlled only by a padlocked gate. The awe that the American team felt on viewing this portal to the "evil empire" faded considerably when one of the locals casually retrieved the key to the padlock from its storage place and crossed over. Then of course everyone had to have their picture taken "in Russia.") Brown trout, sea-trout, the European lake trout, huchen, Atlantic salmon, and even transplanted rainbow trout/steelhead are locally common in the western satellites of the Soviet Union such as Hungary, Rumania, Czechoslovakia, Bulgaria, Poland, Albania, and Yugoslavia, as well as the restive Baltic republics of Estonia, Latvia, and Lithuania.

As glasnost and perestroika began to gain momentum, several regional Soviet fishermen's organizations contacted booking agents and fishing magazines in the United States to try to strike deals and bring American anglers (and their hard currency) to the Soviet Union. At the same time, half a dozen Soviet fly fishermen came to the United States, under the eye of the State Department and the aegis of Trout Unlimited, to fish for trout in New York's Beaverkill River and then the Snake River near Jackson, Wyoming.

The visit was part of a cultural and scientific exchange, to begin the process of swapping data on

A 47-inch, 28-pound taimen caught in the Tiung River, on the Arctic Circle in central Siberia. Photograph by Earl Young.

A fly-caught lenok from Siberia's Olenek River. Earl Young photograph.

trout and salmon fisheries and also to introduce the Soviet sportsmen to the peculiarly American concept of catch-and-release. In the Soviet Union, the very idea of going to the trouble of catching a fish just to release it would send the average sportsman into fits of incredulity. Converting a "gut 'em and eat 'em" ethic to catch-and-release would seem nearly impossible in an economy based on shortages, but Trout Unlimited feels a start has been made. Unless the political situation in the Soviet Union deteriorates to the point where some of its 15 republics secede, leading to open rebellion or civil war (when environmental concerns and sportfishing will go out the window), more and more Westerners will brave Aeroflot's airplanes and scheduling, bad hotels and food, and unpredictable travel conditions to explore the Soviet Union for trout and salmon. Their influence will be felt primarily through the dollars they leave behind, and it won't take long for local outfitters to understand that better fishing leads to more dollars. Capitalism operating for conservation in the heart of communism . . . .

SO THERE ARE at least a few brown trout and rainbows, charr and Atlantic and Pacific salmon, in the corners of the Soviet Union. But what of the vast interior, especially the Siberian wilderness? There, as medieval maps used to put it, lie monsters. Monsters named taimen and huchen, both large, primitive, landlocked Eurasian salmonids of the genus *Hucho*, closely related to the charrs. Biologically, they seem to differ only in their gillrakers, but taimen grow larger and are the more restricted of the two. Taimen are said to be distributed from approximately the Volga River in the west to the Amur River in the east, which amounts to most of Siberia. Huchen, by contrast, are native as far east as Japan—where they are called *ito*, and avidly sought by anglers—and have been stocked as far west as the River Thames in England. (That took place very early in the 20th century; it was thought they might replace the Atlantic salmon that could no longer tolerate London's pollution, but huchen didn't flourish there either. Today, incidentally, a few salmon are beginning to return to the Thames.)

Both huchen and taimen are generally spring-spawning river fish and, except in Japan and perhaps Korea, neither are anadromous. Yet even without the benefit of migrating to large bodies of water where there are vast populations of shrimp, herring or other baitfish, huchen and taimen reportedly can grow at a rate of up to 4 pounds per year, according to British fisheries biologist David Marlborough. There are reliable, if now fairly old, reports of taimen of 150 pounds and huchen of more than 60 pounds. (Japanese biologists write of huchen up to 2 meters, or 80 inches long; if true, those fish must have weighed well over 100 pounds.) Such giants must be exceedingly rare today, as more and more of Siberia has been penetrated and developed, for huchen and taimen both are important food species to the local people. In the Soviet Union there was, maybe still is, something of a commercial fishery for them, although by reputation they are not top-notch table fare.

Few Westerners have caught or even seen these fish, especially taimen, which were slipping into angling folklore when the Soviet Union began to open up. A few years ago, after I had put out feelers in Norway and Sweden inquiring about them, I received a letter from the editor of an East German fishing magazine. In labored English, he explained that he had once been invited to fish in Siberia, where he had seen these giant salmonids, but couldn't land one. (He also wrote of incredible Amur pike in Mongolia that grew to 70 pounds, but that's another story.)

Huchen and taimen are colored like brown trout, but with a decidedly slim and torpedo-like shape, and taimen have distinctly reddish fins. Both *Hucho*s are formidable predators, powerful and aggressive, with mouths full of very un-salmon-like teeth.

Bill Davies, an American married to a Russian woman, has for several years been scouting the Soviet Union for salmon, trout, and taimen. Early on, he asked a Siberian fisherman whether taimen were jumpers. Oh yes, replied the man. And do they jump often, Davies asked? Well, the local said, it depends on how good a shot you are . . . .

The tackle available was of such poor quality that taimen fishing had to be a two-man "sport" in order to even up the odds a bit. One man hooked the fish on rod and line. The second waited for

A lenok of 25 inches, taken in the Tiung River on north-central Siberia. Earl Young photograph.

the fish to jump, then tried to disable it with a blast from a shotgun! The prospects for catch-and-release aren't good.

In 1989, several groups of American fishermen were the first in modern times to get a good crack at taimen fishing. Business commitments kept me from being one of them, to my everlasting regret. After traveling for several days into the heart of Siberia, the group I would have accompanied was met by a large government helicopter—the only kind in the Soviet Union—and a determined and good-natured crew of local guides, who took very good care of them. Altogether they covered miles of water, leapfrogging from river to river and camping on the banks, and the group succeeded in finding taimen. They caught five and released alive all but one small fish; that one went to a taxidermist to serve as the model for fiberglass reproduction "mounts" of taimen. (Thus Western anglers will be able to have a trophy for the wall without actually killing one of these presumably rare fish.) Bob Marriott, a widely traveled angler who owns tackle shops in southern California, took the largest, a 35-pounder, and he said it was the most powerful freshwater fish he had ever encountered.

By comparison, the other native Siberian salmonid, called a lenok, nearly pales in insignificance. It is more widely available, however, as it is much more common and it ranges throughout all of Siberia and into Korea and northern China as well. Lenok are also river fish, but they reach probably only 8 to 10 pounds. They feed on aquatic insects and the like, and most fishermen would identify a lenok as a trout almost immediately, despite its unusually small mouth. The Americans who fished Siberia for taimen caught numbers of lenok using light tackle and techniques, including dry flies, that work for trout all over the world.

CHINA: *Feeding the People*

THE PEOPLE'S REPUBLIC OF CHINA seems to offer the trout or salmon fisherman far less even than the Soviet Union, at least to judge by the sparse information that has trickled out. Frontiers International, an American specialty fishing and shooting travel agency has, to date, sent two one-man survey expeditions into northern China and Manchuria to look for lenok—or any other trout or salmon that might not yet be known in the West—in the Amur River Basin. Both came home disappointed, not only in the fishing but in the primitive services and amenities China can offer the visitor who leaves the beaten path. Chris Child, one of the scouts, found lenok up to 3 pounds (he compared them to brook trout) and was told of "salmon"—almost certainly huchen, possibly taimen—in a nearby river. He scheduled a return visit to check the facts, but flooding and the unusually early onset of winter kept him out. He hasn't been able to go back.

The report of the second man, a Canadian fishing writer and photographer named David Lambroughton, is on my desk before me. He traveled the Zhan and Dulu rivers and claims he was the first Westerner in living memory to enter some of those remote villages. Concerning the fishing, he wrote the following:

"The people who live along these rivers have mouths to feed, including their own. They are fully aware of this source of protein, and they keep the trout ('lennok') and grayling populations well trimmed, primarily with nets. The pre-net size yearlings . . . fare no better, and a common sight along these rivers is to see someone hurrying along the path to home with a basketball-size wad of

The prize of a lifetime—at least for an American angler: a 41-inch Siberian taimen, also caught in the Tiung River. Earl Young photograph.

three- to five-inchers to show for his day of worm fishing."

A billion-plus people in a country the size of the United States inevitably exert certain pressures upon its natural resources. In fact, the population often came between Lambroughton and his mission. On the first morning in a new village—perhaps moving a little slowly after the inevitable welcome feast the night before—he would awaken early and slip off to the stream to fish, however:

"But by the time I was all dressed and ready, and standing there concentrating on my fly or tippet knot or whatever, I'd see little movements out of the corner of my eye. Then more and more, and pretty soon there was every last soul in the village gathered around me—out in the water, even in the trees overhead—watching me with fascination. Whatever trout there were, were long gone."

SRI LANKA, INDIA AND THE HIMALAYAS

WHAT WAS CALLED Ceylon before 1973 was a British tea, rubber, and lumber colony until 1948, so it is no surprise that trout were established there as well. There is only one possible region, the central highlands, whose streams and lakes lie about 7,000 feet above sea level. Sri Lanka, despite the fact that it lies in the Indian Ocean between southern India and the equator, is not all steamy jungles; it is actually a small collection of geographic extremes. Parts of the island verge on the arid while others receive 250 inches of rainfall annually. And up on the Horton Plains, where Californian trout eventually prospered, temperatures may dip below freezing.

The planters and civil servants arranged for the first brown-trout ova to be sent from home in 1882. At first, things looked promising. The fish grew well in those fertile waters and evidently

(above) Stalking trout in Iwate Prefecture. Japan. Kenzo Takano/The Silver Creek Press photograph.
(left) A large brown trout in the Kingdom of Bhutan. Moira O'Connor photograph.

(above) Yamame, the landlocked Japanese cherry trout. Kenzo Takano/The Silver Creek Press photograph.

(left) Iwana, the Japanese mountain charr. Kenzo Takano/The Silver Creek Press photograph.

poaching became a minor problem as the natives developed a taste for trout. But even at that altitude, temperatures proved too high for successful spawning, and the browns dwindled away. Not ones to give up, the colonials formed the Ceylon Fishing Club in 1896, which established a hatchery, persuaded the government to bless its efforts with protected waters and special regulations, and renewed the effort to bestow coldwater angling upon the country. And so in 1899 arrived a shipment of rainbow trout ova from California, fish that could better tolerate the conditions. These fish flourished and—although some of the Brits might secretly have pined for the browns of home—obligingly rose to dry flies for decades. Perhaps the fishing was *too* homelike; reports are that the trout averaged only a pound or so.

The fishery declined after independence, when the servants of the Crown—that is, the most ardent anglers—faded away, but today there is a government-run trout hatchery at Nuwara Eliya augmented by rainbow stock brought from New Zealand in the 1980s. Horton Plains has become a protected nature preserve. And there is at least one factory in Sri Lanka that mass-produces very high quality fishing flies (tied with American materials on Japanese hooks, no less) for export to the United States.

Across the narrow Palk Strait, in India, trout were even more firmly established. Not only was the British presence much greater—India having been more or less the archetypal non-English-speaking Crown colony—there is far more countryside where temperatures and water conditions favor trout. These are almost all in the north of India, from the stunningly beautiful Vale of Kashmir, the high mountain region squeezed between China and Pakistan down along the Himalayas toward Bangladesh. Kashmir was where the white sahibs of the British Raj retreated to escape the stifling heat of the Indian lowlands, and their imprint is still upon the land. Tennis, golf, birding, hiking and climbing, riding, shooting, and even skiing are still available, not to mention trout fishing in snow-fed and spring-fed streams and lakes. The River Lidder and the Trikker became particularly well-known in England as top trout streams for expatriates. Although reports are that today fishing with spinners is the most popular method among Indians to take trout, some of the waters were set aside as fly-only. An ex-major of British armor told me he'd seen signs in the fly-fishing sections that proclaimed TO SPIN IS TO SIN and SPINNING IS SINNING.

Brown trout were planted in many Himalayan streams beginning in about 1900. By then, 40 years after the laborious experiments in Australia, the method of keeping fish eggs alive on extended sea voyages was well established; but there are no navigable rivers that connect Kashmir with the sea, and the long overland trip with the ova must have been difficult. Efforts paid off, however, and only a few years later rainbow trout from America joined the browns. (The rainbows must have been hard-pressed to adapt to the spate rivers of the mountains, which become torrents in the spring runoff. But there are gentler rivers and lakes as well.) British tackle catalogs soon after began advertising special Himalayan trout flies.

Unlike South America, there were three species of native gamefish already in India's rivers when the West arrived. One is the mahseer, a powerful fish that looks like a streamlined and armor-plated carp, which grows to more than 100 pounds. (Mahseer also show up in Pakistan, the mountain principalities, Sri Lanka, and probably Bangladesh.) The other two are trout, at least in appearance and name if not genus. The Indian trout, *Barilus bola*, reportedly looks like a brown; and there is a variant of it called the snow trout that lives in the high, cold lakes.

Trout fishing, or at least fly-fishing, which the Indians regard as nearly one and the same, has become part of the national economy in other ways too. In combination with the Indian culture of backyard metalsmithing (there are Pathan villages in the Punjab that specialize in producing, by hand, high-quality copies of just about every military small arm made in the "civilized" world; the Indian government tends to stay out of there), this heritage of fly-fishing has established a number of companies that make most of the world's inexpensive fly-tying tools.

There are also British-strain brown trout in Pakistan and in the many streams of Nepal, Tibet, Bhutan, and Sikkim, the small nations strung like beads of a necklace along the Himalayas between

India and China. Bhutan is unusual in that the trout were stocked by the Bhutanese themselves, early in the 1950s, at the command of the Royal Family. The fish established themselves very well. There are streams and pools where hundreds of tiny, clearly underfed trout race desperately for every morsel that falls (or is cast) into the water. And there are places—often in the King's own water—where deep-bellied browns of 5 and 6 pounds are not unusual. Until 1974, no Westerners at all were allowed into the kingdom, the Land of the Thunder Dragon, and even today tourism is strictly controlled and limited to about 2,500 visitors annually. It is, as the very few modern anglers who have fished there put it, almost impossibly exotic—a 7th-century way of life preserved nearly intact. Modern contradictions have appeared, however; in a devoutly Buddhist country, how does one explain fishing? In a very neat tour de force, Mike McLelland, the Los Angeles entrepreneur who has the exclusive on fishing tours in Bhutan, received the blessings of the all-powerful lamas by explaining to them that modern fly-fishing for trout is based upon the concept of releasing the catch *alive*, and unharmed. They decided that not only would such fishing be allowed, they even gave their blessing to another project that is getting underway in the kingdom in 1990—a small "factory" that is tying flies for the American market.

JAPAN: *Many Anglers, Little Opportunity*

BASEBALL AND GOLF were not the only Western pastimes that caught on big in Japan. While there has always been a native fishing tradition, for food and recreation—embracing, among other things, a form of fly-fishing using long bamboo poles to skate tiny dry flies across stream pools—trout fishing, especially with flies, has become a prestige sport. Tackle companies bring in British and American experts to teach popular casting seminars, and sales of expensive imported rods, reels, and fly-tying materials and tools continue to boom (aided, of course, by the powerful Japanese economy and high standard of living). Unfortunately, while sea fishing grounds are fairly plentiful off the Japanese islands, trout waters are rare on the islands, at least in comparison to the natural bounty of North America or Scandinavia, and the best fishing is either very remote or controlled and thus fairly expensive.

Despite the recent surge in popularity, "modern" fly-fishing arrived in Japan more or less when brown trout from America were introduced in 1892. This was in Lake Chuzenji, in the central mountains near Nikko City, which now is one of the country's top angling spots. Brown trout and rainbows—*nijimasu*—of nearly 40 inches have reportedly been taken there, which are large by any standard. The rainbows were brought into Japan, also from America, as early as 1877, and brook trout (from Maine—*kawamasu* in Japanese) first arrived in 1902. All three species are now widely propagated in hatcheries throughout Japan, but only the brook trout and a few browns seem able to hold over and reproduce naturally in any numbers. The rainbow has probably become the most popular hatchery trout now, and the very small population of rainbows that have gone wild, in northern Japan, are highly esteemed as rare gamefish.

One reason for the difficulty the exotics have had in getting established on their own is that many Japanese streams flow fast and furiously, especially for rainbows. Another is simply competition from the native salmonid species, who are better adapted. The most popular of these, at least from

The yamame trout is distinguished by its unique plum-colored oval markings. Kenzo Takano/The Silver Creek Press photograph.

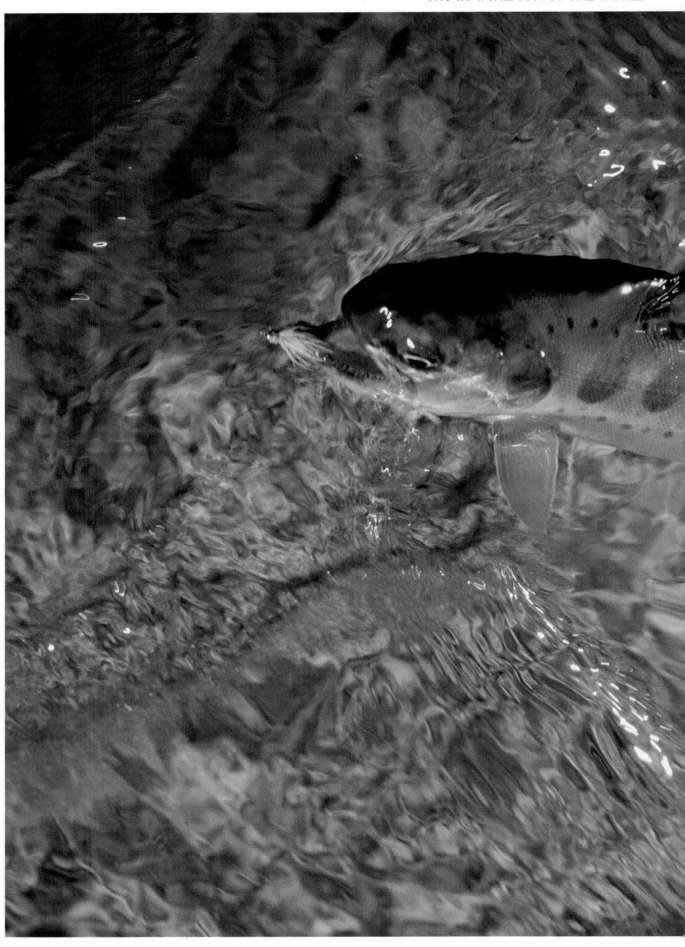

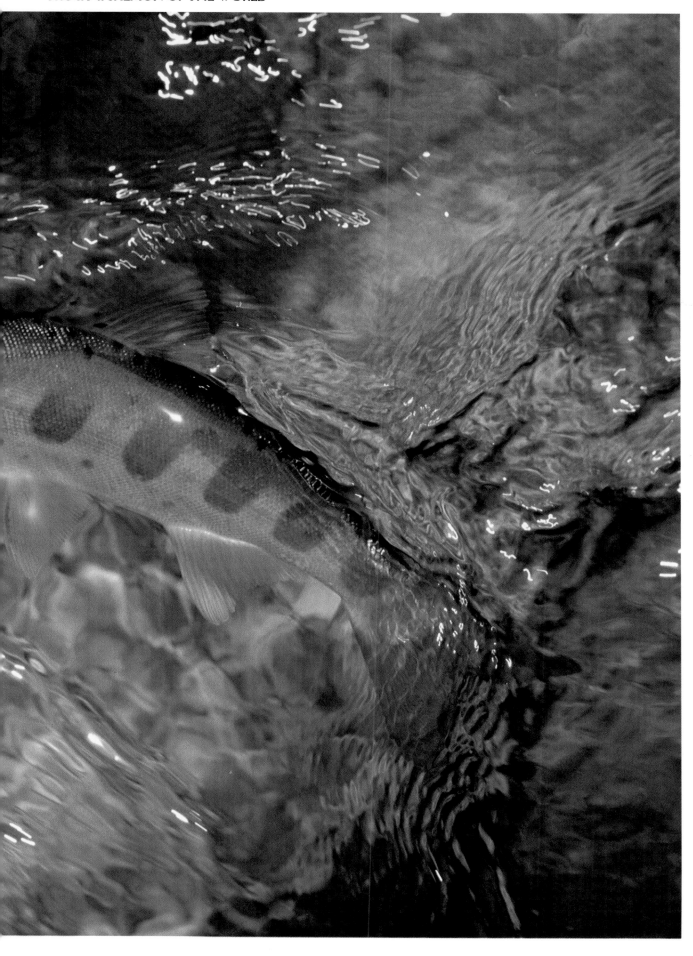

the fly fisherman's viewpoint, is the *yamame* trout, which is in fact a landlocked subspecies of the *sakuramasu*, or cherry salmon. Highly prized, these delicate (and hard to release) gamefish rarely reach a foot in length and, even as adults, bear unique plum-colored ovals on their flanks that look like fat parr marks. The sea-run form, which dies after spawning and is fairly common in the rivers that flow off Hokkaido (the northern island) into the Sea of Japan, may grow to twice that size. The largest native Japanese salmonid, however, is the carnivorous and spring-spawning *ito*, or huchen. As mentioned, there is a record of a Japanese ito 6 1/2 feet long, but today fish of only half that size are rare, even among the huchen of the northeast coast that swim out to sea to mature.

In addition to the exotic American brook trout (and even lake trout, a few of which were brought to Japan in 1966 and then planted in Lake Chusenji), there are also a handful of charr subspecies, including the Dolly Varden, that are native to Japan and the nearby Asian continent. Differentiating between certain charrs is a matter that can be resolved only on the dissection table, but the two most important as gamefish in Japan are the *amemasu* and the *iwana*. Both are fall spawners that live in very cold water, either the headwaters of mountain streams or the bottoms of lakes or river pools. Although 15 to 18 inches is normally the maximum for either fish, individuals of twice that size have been caught in some of the deep, cold lakes. There is also a sea-run form of amemasu that may grow to 30 inches or so as well.

As Japan is essentially a coldwater archipelago, it is no surprise that the country's rivers host a number of true salmons, many of them also found on the opposite shore of the Pacific, in North America. These include all five of the Pacific species—king (chinook), silver (coho), sockeye (red), humpback (pink), and chum (dog) salmon—as well as steelhead, the anadromous form of the rainbow trout.

Down Under

AUSTRALIA: *The Greatest Challenge*

TROUT FISHING Down Under is alive and very well, thanks again to the transplantational urges of colonizing Britishers—and, in this case, of a few Americans as well. Small parts of Australia (the planet's most arid continent) and nearly all of New Zealand enjoy the sort of temperate climate, clean water, and good insect hatches—and the reasonably healthy ecosystem that allows all these factors to exist—lead salmonids to flourish. And of course those nations were important parts of the British Empire. How these fish arrived in Australia perfectly illustrates the sort of personal vision and initiative of England's citizens that made her the world's pre-eminent industrial power.

Tasmania's trout fishery—mostly browns, migratory and riverine, and some rainbows, plus a few brook trout that originally hailed from Maine—is little known in the United States, yet it deserves to be. The trout are widespread on the island, but fishing is concentrated in several large lakes and in the central highlands. There, hundreds of small, clear, cold, shallow lakes lie scattered across a landscape that progresses from dense eucalyptus forests, home to wallabies, devils, and kookaburras, to barely vegetated semi-desert that turns so inhospitable in winter that Australia's Antarctic training station is located there. Tasmania, Australia's southernmost state, is as far south as New England is north, and their seasons mirror each other closely, but of course at opposite ends of the calendar. Tasmania's climate, however, is affected by the ocean currents and the eternal winds of the Southern Ocean and the polar ice.

The trout are, of course, exotics—the rainbows came from New Zealand. First to arrive, however, were the browns, English River Itchen, Wye and Wick (both Thames tributaries) natives that were finally delivered alive to the island in 1864 by a persistent man named James A. Youl, who was later

knighted for it. The 23-year history of the attempt to introduce trout and salmon into Australia was unusually well documented in the British press; some of the periodicals that covered the story are still published today. It was a feat unlike any other in fisheries management, before or since.

Under the aegis of the Acclimatisation Society of Victoria and the Salmon Commission of Tasmania, three attempts to ship fertilized eggs or fry to Australia failed because the 16,000 mile trip across the equator without artificial refrigeration simply took too long in sailing ships. (One batch was sent aboard a steamship, but the vessel proceeded under sail because it was feared the vibration of the engine would harm the fish ova—leading one to wonder what human steamship passengers had to endure.) But James Youl persisted. Eventually, learning from his failures and with the advice of scientists who had moved trout around Europe, he developed a method that worked. He designed special pine boxes filled with layers of charcoal, crushed ice, and water-soaked moss, in which the eggs were cradled. The boxes would then be covered with ice blocks; and the meltwater from these blocks would percolate down through holes drilled in the boxes, thereby cooling and washing the ova.

Temperature and moisture were only part of the problem, however; a serious overage in sailing time meant the voyage would exceed the eggs' gestation period—even as lengthened so drastically by the low temperatures of their shipboard environment—and they would hatch and die within their travel containers. Merely to get fresh ova from healthy, about-to-spawn fish at the right time was no small feat. Frank Buckland, who obtained the Itchen eggs, wrote of struggling with heavy nets in the stream and "getting thoroughly wet into the bargain." And this was in January.

The entire icehouse built aboard the clipper *Norfolk* for the project was reported to take up 56 tons by volume. Having begun loading some 3,000 trout eggs and 100,000 Atlantic salmon eggs— in 180 of these special boxes under 9 feet of ice blocks—only three days before, the ship left London on January 21, 1864, and docked in Melbourne on April 15. Eleven salmon crates stayed there; all the rest were transferred to the *Victoria* (at the time, Australia's one and only warship), southbound for Hobart, the capital of Tasmania. There they went onto a barge that was towed up the Derwent River by a small steamer. At the falls on the Derwent, porters carried the boxes on foot the final few miles up a tributary called the River Plenty. At last, 91 days after the voyage began, the eggs were carefully placed into prepared breeding boxes and the waiting and watching began. (The place is now known as the Salmon Ponds of Plenty and is maintained as a historic site.) Published estimates were that about 300 trout and 35,000 salmon ova had survived the trip.

The timing could not have been better; as the temperature of the eggs came up, the first trout hatched on May 4, the first salmon on the fifth. Back in Melbourne, those salmon began to hatch on May 7. There was jubilation among the Commissioners and the Society members. Medals were struck, plaques erected, ship's officers and fish handlers praised, and cheers issued forth from newspapers and sporting magazines in Australia and back in England. For two years, breeding stock were carefully nurtured. A few fish were released and took up residence.

A second shipment of eggs, this time of migratory (sea-trout) as well as brown trout and salmon, came from England aboard the *Lincolnshire* in 1866 to the Ponds of Plenty. These survivors fared well also; the Commission was then able to plant more fish in the wild and to improve their captive

A beautifully marked (but small) wild Tasmanian brown trout.

(above) A classic freestone trout stream— but it's not Montana or New Zealand, it's Natal, South Africa. Photograph courtesy of Frontiers International.

(right) A fabulous South Island brown trout. Photograph by Tom Montgomery.

brood stock at the same time. And in that year the first brown-trout ova were sent from Tasmania back up north to Melbourne; trout had arrived in mainland Australia.

Unfortunately, the Melbourne salmon were never seen again after they had been released into Badger Creek. Migratory fish have a disconcerting habit of simply swimming downstream and away, leaving their protectors to wonder—in this case for several years, as there were no previous salmon to mature and return only one year later—about their fate. Non-migratory or riverine species just stay put and can be watched daily. In Tasmania, salmon and then sea-trout were both released into the Derwent and several tributaries, and all seemed to go well; big, silver-colored salmonids began to come back upstream to spawn. A 28-pound fish caught in the Huon River was thought to be a salmon. It was almost certainly an oversize sea-trout, for these salmon never did

A Kiwi brown taken on the North Island—"only" 4 pounds. The water clarity and vivid colors are typical. Tom Montgomery photograph.

"take" in Australian waters, despite more shipments of ova from Britain in 1884, 1885, and 1876.

Curiously, Atlantic salmon have never been successfully planted in the Southern Hemisphere, whether in Australia, New Zealand, Tierra del Fuego and mainland Patagonia, or the Falkland Islands. (There is, as noted elsewhere in this book, some talk of trying again in Tierra del Fuego's Rio Grande. If it happens, it will almost certainly be a waste of time and money.) Sea-trout, *Salmo trutta*, fare very well; their very close relative *Salmo salar*, the Atlantic salmon, simply vanishes. A partial exception is the landlocked form of *S. salar*, which has become a famous gamefish in southern Chile and Argentina and is established, but far less well known, in New Zealand. The most logical explanation for this was first offered by G. Stokeli, author of *Fresh Water Fishes of New Zealand*. He pointed out that the sea around his country averages about 10 degrees warmer than the waters off Scotland; the coldest latitude New Zealand can muster is about 50 degrees south, while the British Isles only start at about 50 degrees north and their best salmon water is another 400 miles closer to the Pole. Scandinavia is even farther to the north and its water colder yet. Evidently, the habitat in the Southern Hemisphere is unsuitable for a species with such narrowly defined needs.

Today, the Tasmanian brown trout is a handsome creature, seemingly more wild and pugnacious, predatory yet secretive than normal. The big ones are strong and solid, and their colors seem sharper and more brilliant—the yellow belly more red-gold, the spots larger and brighter. These are among the most memorable trout I know, and "Polaroiding" for them, in those high lakes, is the most challenging trout fishing, more difficult even than fly-fishing the renowned spring creeks of Yellowstone Country. The lake water is still and often clear as air; along with the fly, the line and leader sit up in plain view like signposts warning the trout that all is not proper here. More often than not a knifelike wind is streaming across that high country, creating a disturbance on the water's surface that hides the angler's tools, but that also makes casting and presenting the fly tricky.

The challenge is that, as in New Zealand, under ideal conditions this is sight-fishing—stalking individual fish that are feeding or cruising in plain view. And usually the big browns are right on the very verges of these lakes, almost literally on the shore itself, with not only their dorsal fins but sometimes their entire backs out of the water, nosing about in the high green grass of dry land for freshwater shrimps, snails, and bugs.

In this case they have to be approached from the water side, with great stealth and cunning, and the fly dropped just so in front of their noses. In such an exposed position, the fish are extremely shy. Do everything right, factor in a dose of luck, and a wild trout of as much as 10 pounds or more may explode out of the shallows and streak for deeper water, straining against your fragile tippet.

AND WHAT of those brown trout ova that were shipped from the Ponds of Plenty to Melbourne in 1866? That first batch hatched successfully, but heavy rains flooded the hatching boxes and washed away the fry. Five more transplants from Tasmania all failed in succession for one reason or another. The last one, however, may not have failed; what happened was that someone stole the fry out of the hatchery. Since they were far too small to eat, they may well have been released into the wild surreptitiously, and this was perhaps the first "successful" planting of trout into the state of Victoria. At any rate, while shipments of eggs continued to arrive from down south, by 1870 there were

Tom Montgomery photographed this silver rainbow on the Rangitikei River of the North Island.

credible reports of mature trout in Victorian streams. Whether they were the stolen trout or those that had been washed away in the flood in 1866 can't be known and in fact doesn't matter. Trout had been established, if in small numbers, on the Australian mainland.

The struggle to widen the stocking went on, however. Members of the Acclimatisation Society Council sought to improve their hatchery situation with more and better ponds, but luck continued to run against them. Weather, silt, poachers, and even incompetent fish-handlers repeatedly reduced their brood stock to very low levels. Without the now-annual boxes of ova from Tasmania, where the trout had settled in like natives, the project would have foundered early on. Small numbers of fry were distributed widely throughout the state, when available, but trout couldn't really be said to have settled in until about the turn of the century. Finally a proper hatchery was built in the

Zoological Gardens in Melbourne and, in 1909, 40,000 brown trout ova were hatched there, and another 30,000 Loch Leven browns, the silvery Scottish strain. They were over the hump.

Still, it didn't get all that much easier. Having failed with Atlantic salmon, the Society turned to the Pacific species. Twenty-five thousand chinook eggs from northern California died en route in 1874. Two years later they tried again, with twice as many ova, and most of them survived, at least for a while. Jack Ritchie, in his excellent modern book *The Australian Trout*, describes the tremendous efforts of Sir Samuel Wilson, a transplanted Irishman who'd become wealthy and a member of Australia's Parliament. He personally managed to carry—by rail car, wagon, horseback and, finally on foot—water cans of these salmon fry overland all the way to the Snowy River, in northeastern Victoria. And after all that superhuman effort, none of them survived to spawn either.

Now, there are in fact small populations of chinook salmon in Victoria and Atlantic salmon in New South Wales, but they are nearly all put-and-take hatchery fish, restocked annually. The only naturally reproducing "salmon" in Australia is a tropical saltwater gamefish called the threadfin salmon, which is not a *Salmo* at all.

Today, brown and rainbow trout thrive in many streams and ponds in southeastern Australia, particularly from the New England mountain range in New South Wales on down through the Great Snowy Mountains south of Canberra and into the alpine regions of the state of Victoria. Every year a few fish of 8 to 10 pounds or so are written up in the angling press, but in truth, on the mainland trout are far overshadowed by the spectacular ocean fishing that surrounds the entire continent. Still, trout have been transplanted all the way across the great central desert into Western Australia, in the extreme southwestern corner, between Perth and Albany.

Ironically, Australia, the site of the most difficult artificial transplant of salmonids ever to succeed, began to outlaw the importation of exotic species sooner and more comprehensively than other nations. The trout was a benign immigrant that happened to slot easily into what is one of the most unusual ecologies on earth; it created no problems and displaced no native fish. But Australia has gotten far less pleasure from the rabbits and other species that were also imported and that became major pests. However, these hard-earned lessons didn't keep Aussie government officers from going to great trouble and expense to introduce "their" rainbow trout into—of all places—the central mountain streams of Papua New Guinea. And this took place very recently, in the 1960s and '70s. The Australian Fisheries Council, evidently still impressed with trout, did not outlaw their further importation until 1970; and Papua New Guinea gained its independence from Australia in 1975. Ritual tribal warfare, not to mention head-hunting, have pretty much disappeared even from the remote Central Highlands of PNG, but it is still one of the wildest regions left on earth and trout fishing there must rank as adventure of the first order.

AFRICA: *Something Different*

AS ANOTHER FORMER British stomping ground, parts of the Dark Continent have also received transplanted trout. More surprising, at least to those who aren't aware of the full range of geography and climate that Africa offers, is the fact that trout have done fairly well there. And furthermore, there are even native European brown trout, in the Atlas Mountains of Morocco (where there is also

Angler removes his fly with surgeon's forceps: a Young River, South Island rainbow, photographed by Tom Montgomery.

A rainbow from the North Island caught in its spawning time. Tom Montgomery photograph.

alpine skiing) that lie just across the Strait of Gibraltar from Spain. The trout region extends from the northeastern quadrant—Kenya, plus some small pockets of fish in Ethiopia and even the Sudan—down to the southern tip of the continent—South Africa, Botswana, Zimbabwe—with Tanzania and Mozambique included along the way. Throughout this vast area are highlands where the average temperatures are far lower than in the rest of Africa and there are free-flowing streams supported by springs and adequate rainfall. (Nineteen-thousand-foot Mount Kilimanjaro and several other peaks in Kenya, Uganda, and Tanzania are permanently snow-capped even though they all lie within a few miles of the equator.) And even at a mile or so above sea level, Africa produces more than enough crustaceans, forage fish, and aquatic and terrestrial insects to feed trout very well.

Africa's political upheavals have affected every part of the continent and everything living there, directly or indirectly, including trout—and trout fishermen. From one year to the next, a drainage may be clearcut or burned, a border changed, or a river poached off by hungry grenade-throwing troops or by a farmer feeding his wives and children. A friend who was the North American Bureau chief for South Africa's Argus newspapers told me of fishing in the Rhodesian uplands near the Mozambique border (before it became Zimbabwe) armed to the teeth, with one eye out not for animals but for guerrillas. Things are quiet there now, and there is reportedly good fishing for not only browns and rainbows but also some brook trout.

Kenya and South Africa, where the European influence was strongest, are still the most settled and the least physically polluted and damaged of Africa's "trout country" but South Africa's time of upheaval may yet come. Anyone who wants to travel to any part of Africa to fish for trout, or anything else, would do well to inquire into present conditions first.

According to British angling expert Tony Pawson, a Maj. Grogan imported brown trout and rainbow ova to Kenya in 1905 and released the fry into streams in the Aberdare Mountains north and west of Nairobi. Other English fish followed in 1907, and a shipment, again of browns and rainbows, arrived from South Africa in 1910. Both species were apparently well established then already. There are accounts of trophies of 5, 6, and 7 pounds throughout the 1920s and '30s, when a government hatchery was also augmenting natural reproduction, but then and now trout of about a pound were normal. By northern standards, these are marginal fisheries; although the trout propagate and grow quickly, they do not grow very large and they don't live very long. A few stillwater fisheries have been created, mostly for tourists, by dams. Some rivers are patrolled against poachers by game scouts; others, especially on the wild Aberdare Plateau and down in Tanzania, can actually be dangerous to fish because of buffalo, elephants, and lions. Unlike the brown bears of coastal Alaska, these animals are more interested in the fishermen than in the fish; at least trout streams don't have crocodiles.

South Africa began to get imported browns and rainbows in the 1890s from England and Scotland and America. They have become a small but important part of the sporting life there, especially in the Drakensberg Mountains of Natal Province, where there are many miles of good trout streams and fish often reach 3 pounds. A few coastal streams of the far south are cold enough to support trout, but near Johannesburg most trout are in manmade ponds above 4,000 feet of elevation. Often the fisheries are part of guesthouses or small hotels. Trout were eventually carried to much of the rest of South Africa by enthusiastic volunteers, whose labors in some cases must have rivalled those of the Australians, but in those places trout have not fared so well. (American largemouth and smallmouth bass have generally done far better in South Africa.) There are at least three federal trout hatcheries, which stock those ponds and maintain populations throughout the country.

NEW ZEALAND: 'Angler's Eldorado'
THIS SEA-GIRT small country, the sheep-growing Switzerland of the Southern Hemisphere, is a haven—or perhaps a heaven—for all sorts of gamefish, and thus all sorts of fishermen. It was the best-selling American author Zane Grey who tipped us off, in 1926, when his book about New Zealand, *Tales of the Angler's Eldorado*, was published. It is true that Grey was a pioneering big-game

fisherman, but he was no less avid a trout and steelhead man too, and he wrote glowingly of New Zealand's rainbows. Today the average size of those trout has dropped, but it is still marvelous by most standards and the setting is unsurpassed anywhere on earth. I believe New Zealand to be the only place on earth that I have never heard a single complaint about from a traveling fisherman.

Rainbows up to about 7 pounds predominate on the more populated and pastoral North Island, and browns on the wilder, mountainous South Island; some of them still reach 12 pounds or more. Throughout the entire country, both kinds of trout often seem to be bursting with life, brilliantly colored, hard-fighting, and clearly as healthy and well-fed as wild animals can be. Their rivers and lakes too seem almost otherwordly in their beauty, whether they be the high alpine brooks of the colder southern latitudes or the gentler and more wooded streams of the north.

Rainbow trout ova arrived in New Zealand from California in 1883; after hatching they were planted in Taupo, the tremendous lake that lies dead-center in the North Island, and they have been a huge success ever since, spreading first into the Tongariro River and throughout that watershed and then being carried all over the rest of the country. (There was a sign in Turangi, the town on Taupo's south end, that proclaims it is the "Trout Capital of the World.") American brook trout were introduced into Lake Taupo also, in 1952, but they fared no better than they did in Australia.

New Zealand's brown trout are Tasmanian; that is, British Thames and Itchen fish that came by way of that first successful shipment to Australia on the *Norfolk*. The Acclimatisation Societies of both Otago and Christchurch (every right-thinking colonial municipality had such a group) each brought home to the South Island 800 brown trout ova in 1867. More than 100 years later, the South Island, which holds more than half the land mass of New Zealand, is still heavily forested, very lightly populated, and incredibly rugged and beautiful. Rudyard Kipling—another one of those Brits traveling to seek his fortune—called it the eighth wonder of the world. The Southern Alps, which exceed 10,000 feet in a few spots, form the spine of the island, and off their slopes run literally thousands of streams and creeks and even a few large glaciers (the southern tip of the island is only about 1,500 miles from Antarctica). Trout habitat like this, and in this scope, exists in only a very few places on the globe, and perhaps nowhere else is it still as ideal for trout. For the angler to see much of it, however, requires deep pockets—with which to hire a helicopter and guide.

Wherever brown trout and rainbows live without stress in streams that flow into the sea, a few fish eventually become at least semi-migratory, whether anadromous strains have been stocked or not. The South Island is less than 100 miles wide in places, and the ocean is never very far away; consequently there are sea-trout and reportedly a few steelhead rainbows there as well. And, although they have historically not been popular with visiting anglers, New Zealand also has excellent runs of wild salmon, Pacific chinook originally brought from northern California and known locally as quinnat. Unlike the 70-plus-pound monsters of the Kenai and other Alaskan rivers, however, these chinook rarely exceed 20 pounds. In the South Island they come ashore, especially in the big, braided east-coast rivers, which are usually overlooked by trout fishermen whose heads have been turned by tales of the much smaller and remote waters.

The failure to implant a true sea-going strain of Atlantic salmon has long been a disappointment to "acclimatisation" minded New Zealanders. It certainly wasn't for lack of proper habitat or food, or even for lack of trying. For a century, beginning in 1868, there have been many attempts with At-lantic salmon fry hatched from ova obtained in Scotland, the Canadian Maritimes, the Rhine River, Sweden, and even Poland. When they were released into rivers with no lakes at one end and the sea at the other, the fingerlings simply swam away, never to be seen again. The government also tried millions of fry of the so-called Te Anau salmon, anadromous Atlantics, that had been planted in that huge lake at the south end of the South Island and become landlocked there, but they didn't revert to their former sea-going habits either. Presently there are small but well-established populations of landlocks that reach 2 or 3 pounds in the lake systems of the South Island, but even the locals hardly know it, and often identify them as particularly hard-fighting brown trout.

Frankenstein's Fish

by Ted Williams

IT STRIKES ROBERT H. SMITH and me that those who pursue and manage fish in these United States are forgetting things, such as what fish are and why they are important. Take, for example, our favorite fish—trout. God made them last, someone told me when I was a child, after He had practiced on all the others. But now fish managers are making them over, and everyone, save me and Robert H. Smith, thinks it's swell. "They're Making Tomorrow's Fish Today," effused the January 1986 *Field & Stream*, a magazine that once (in the 19th century) dedicated itself to "a refined taste in natural objects."

Robert H. Smith is a retired wildlife biologist who lives in Central Point, Oregon, and has written *Native Trout of North America* (Frank Amato Publications, Portland, Oregon)—a handsome, intelligent, badly needed book that isn't selling. Smith and I maintain life-lists of wild fish species and strains we have caught, held, photographed and, usually, released. Not that we mind exercising lunkers, but the trophy that most often pleases us measures under 8 inches. In salmonids, alas, Smith is way ahead of me, having taken every species and subspecies native to North America except three— Maine's blueback trout, the Sunapee golden trout, and Ontario's aurora trout.

The other day he was moaning and groaning about how all the trout streams in the West have been fouled with hatchery genes. You hike 10 miles up a canyon only to find that the pure strain of cutthroats you thought persisted in the headwaters has been hybridized to extinction by domestic rainbows whose distant wild ancestors hailed from the Pacific Coast. I laughed a patient, indulgent laugh, a laugh born of three decades of plodding the silty, put-and-take runoff of the Northeast, beginning with the Aberjona River—the ditched conduit that drains the world-famous toxic dumps of Woburn, Massachusetts. No danger of hybridization—or even reproduction—in such "trout streams."

These days I catch hatchery trout only by accident—genetic wrecks that penetrate, like coliform bacteria, to the forgotten rills I find by first locating the state stocking route and then proceeding upstream and in the opposite direction. Recently I cut open one of these fish to see what it had been feeding on; it had been feeding on cigarette butts.

Hatchery trout are everything real trout are not. They are selected not to consume live fauna but processed pellets, not to thrive amid clean gravel, rocks and brush, but in filthy, crowded cement troughs that wear away scales and fins. The flaglike dorsal, because it is on top, is the one fin that cannot be worn away. But hatchery trout tend to this themselves, nipping any dorsal in sight so that virtually all become fleshy, withered stumps. Walk along a wild trout stream and fish will streak for cover. Walk along a hatchery raceway and fish will streak to your side in the hope of getting fed. After years of inbreeding, hatchery trout tend to be deformed. Gill covers don't fit, jaws are bent, tails pinched. They are wriggling sausages flung to the public like gurry flung to gulls, and consumed as raucously. In my state, Massachusetts, some stocked trout actually bear tags that may be exchanged for prizes. And Smith thinks he has it tough.

A while back, Bob Smith was plying hallowed Western water for steelhead, but had caught only what managers call the "hatchery product." "Rubber trout!" he snorted. "I had just pulled in one of the poor creatures, about a foot long, fin-clipped and otherwise mutilated. It lay there in the shallows on its side, leering at me in a lipless grin. Its maxillary was gone.

" 'My God,' I thought, 'is this the reward for a day on the stream? Is this what my license money supports?' "

Yes, Bob, it is. But it gets worse, much worse. Consider, for example, brown trout, walleye, muskellunge, and striped bass. Rarely are wild populations fished out, even inside cities. All four species are (or were) prized gamefish, not because they fight well—although they do—but because they are moody and selective, a real challenge to outwit. Even skilled, patient fishermen who have taken the time to learn their ways don't fill up the cooler every time out.

So the managers rose to their own challenge. Rather than make smarter fishermen they made dumber fish. They crossed a brook trout, actually a species of char, with a brown trout, a true trout, to get a garish, idiot fish that gobbles everything in sight. "Tiger trout" they call it. The public snatches them out as fast as the managers dump them in, which translates in the lingo to "a good return." "It has very little holdover potential because it's stupid," declares Charlie Heartwell of West Virginia's Department of Natural Resources. "Fishermen," he says, "really like it."

"Saugeyes" which are manufactured by scrambling the genes of sauger and walleye, can be caught even by those who haven't had or taken the time to practice on either of the canny, coy parent fish. And the muskie, once considered the "trophy of a lifetime," may be had in just a weekend or two now that it has been hybridized with the gluttonous and indiscriminate pike. "Tiger muskie" they call the widely stocked concoction.

Then there is the "wiper" (a.k.a. whiterock bass, sunshine bass, and hybrid bass), the most popular illegitimate of them all, springing from the forced union of the freshwater white bass and the anadromous striper. It is, I am told, a real management triumph, all the rage in at least 20 states. It is fast-growing, hard-fighting, imbued with the typical "hybrid vigor." It has made slow fishing fast, eating thousands of tons of "worthless" threadfin and gizzard shad and thereby converting them to firm, tasty gamefish flesh. If one respects the natural world, one perceives in wiper production something intrusive, insulting, and depraved. Here, briefly, is how it's done:

First you capture migrating male white bass by stunning them with an electric shocker. Since whites spawn earlier than stripers, you have to keep them in a holding pond. When the stripers start showing in the rivers you stun and capture cows, whose eggs, unlike those of whites, are large, easily handled and don't stick to everything they touch. You ripen the cows by injecting them with human chorionic gonodatropin hormone and run a catheter up their ovaries to check egg development. Then you squeeze them until their eggs squirt into a pan. Finally, you wring the milt out of 10 to 15 whites and mix it in.

THERE IS scarcely an unnatural coupling of fish gametes that has not been accomplished by some manager somewhere: largemouth/smallmouth bass; striper/yellow bass; white perch/striper; blue/channel catfish; corvina/weakfish; red/black drum; rainbow/brown trout; rainbow/cutthroat trout; lake/brook trout; European/Asian carp; redear/green sunfish; bluegill sunfish/largemouth bass; and longear sunfish/largemouth bass. "Sometimes I think they come up with these things and try to find a place to put them," remarks New York fisheries biologist Ed Van Put.

A Wisconsin manager told me this: "One of our guys wanted to hybridize brown trout and Atlantic salmon. He said he wanted to create a fish that fought like an Atlantic salmon but stayed where you stocked it, like a brown. And I said, 'But what if the opposite happens and you get a fish that fights like a brown and wanders like a salmon?'"

I felt a little surge of hope and congratulated the manager, but that very afternoon I learned that such a creature—called a "Sam-Brown"—had been hatched in Connecticut. "Kind of a little attempt to see what would happen with them," the official explained. But the program has been dropped— temporarily, he expects—and not for any of the plentiful right reasons. Only because Connecticut "didn't have the personnel."

One "advantage" nearly all the hybrids have is their ability to withstand pollution. "Fishery personnel must produce fish strains [hybrids] that tolerate deteriorating habitat," instructs the October 1986 *Sport Fishing Institute Bulletin*. Must they indeed? What are they telling the public when they do? It would be one thing if managers, as a group, made any significant noise about pollution, but they do not. So the message is clear: Don't worry if you foul the environment and wipe out clean-water fish; we'll just make foul-water fish.

Another "advantage" of hybrids, say managers, is that they tend to be sterile, much like mules, and therefore may be shut off if they start messing up ecosystems. But, having worked as a hired barker for the managers, I know how they think. Messing up ecosystems has never been something they chew their nails about. Even today they are seeding habitats with alien species they hope will work out like pheasants but, more likely, will work out like starlings. For managers, the real advantage of hybrid sterility is that it keeps them on the payroll. Hybrids must constantly be cranked out; they cannot simply be planted and forgotten.

Actually, some of the hybrids are turning out to be not that sterile. Wiper reproduction in the wild—probably backcrossing with whites—has been documented in Texas. When wipers were backcrossed with stripers in the laboratory, nearly 50 percent of the progeny were badly deformed. What happens if wipers transmit their twisted, nonmigratory genes to wild striped bass, a species very much in trouble throughout its natural range?

It gets worse still. Bob Smith perceives the little golden trout of the high Sierra Nevada to be "the most gorgeously colored" trout in the world. "Never," he recalls, on beholding his first specimen, "had I seen such intense blends of greens, carmines, yellows and black, yet it wasn't garish; nothing clashed, and the total impression was exquisite beauty beyond words." When the managers brought goldens down from the mountains to the hatcheries, the trout faded. So the managers made "goldens" of their own.

They used various techniques. In a tray of several thousand domestic rainbow trout fingerlings, West Virginia hatchery workers found a single washed-out mutant lacking in melanin. By fertilizing its eggs with milt from normal domestic rainbows, they established a line of bilious mutants. The first batch was ready for stocking in 1963—which happened to be the state's centennial year—so the beast was called the "West Virginia Centennial golden trout." All manner of hype was pumped out on the new fish. The legislature passed a law forbidding hatchery personnel to let it fall into the clutches of out-of-state fish-culturists. Today West Virginia stocks about 130,000 a year on a put-and-take basis.

A similar mutant called the "palomino trout" is stocked by Pennsylvania. "People seem to like it," says state fisheries technician Charles Cooper. "They're kind of thrown in as a specialty-type fish just to attract the angler's attention."

Utah does it differently and with different motives. The Division of Wildlife Resources mass-produces albinos—real ones, with pink eyes. Management coordinator Glenn Davis explains: "What they do is mix them in the loads. The angler can see the albinos in the stream, and it kind of cuts down on the complaints that we're not stocking enough fish."

Not surprisingly, the melanin-deprived rainbows are light-sensitive. They do not feed or behave naturally, and survival in the real world is even more fleeting than it is for regular domestics. "They were popular because they shine out like beacons," says Connecticut fish manager James Moulton. "But if we can see them, so can every otter, mink and everything else that's trying to catch them." Is that why Connecticut quit stocking them? "No," says Moulton. "Someone stole the brood stock."

MOST DENIZENS of this planet have in each cell two sets of chromosomes. Sperm and eggs must therefore reduce their chromosomes to a single set to prevent the embryo from having four. But fish managers have learned how to foil this process by shocking eggs with heat, hydrostatic pressure or chemicals just as they are about to shed one chromosome set (which in the egg happens after fertilization). Shocking results in hatchlings with three sets of chromosomes.

Why would anyone want to do this? Well, you have to think like a manager. First, "triploid fish" as these freaks are called, are sterile; their odd number of chromosomes cannot synapse in natural gametogenesis. Second, the gonads are structurally deformed, and nutrients that would normally go into their development are rechanneled to body bulk. Bigness, in and for itself. That is what the angling public demands, and that is what the managers serve up.

Triploid work is under way or about to start almost everywhere one looks. Already Wisconsin and Michigan are dumping triploid chinook salmon into the Great Lakes. Normal, diploid chinooks—which don't belong in the lakes anyway and are disrupting the spawning of brown and rainbow trout (which also don't belong in the lakes)—are huge by any standard, sometimes growing to 40 pounds, at which point they spawn and die. But the triploids, which don't spawn, may reach 100 pounds. With more time to soak up DDT and PCBs, they will be more safely stuffed for the wall than the oven. On the outside, triploid salmon look like diploids; to prevent any suspicion that nature had a hand in their production, the managers chop off their adipose fins and run coded wires through their noses.

The mad science breeds its own momentum. Triploids make possible a new line of hybrids. For instance, coho salmon and chinooks have different numbers of chromosomes in the two sets, so if you mix the species the chromosomes don't pair right and you get gross deformities. But if you make a triploid, with two sets of maternal chromosomes (one that doesn't pair and therefore retains unscrambled information) and one of the paternal, you get a fish that will survive.

And now researchers have perfected a technique to destroy genetic material with ultraviolet light. They can strip fish sperm of its single set of chromosomes, use it to fertilize eggs, shock the eggs to prevent the expulsion of the second set of female chromosomes, and produce fertile fish with two sets of the maternal chromosomes—clones. That is not the worst of it. Female salmon are being shot full of testosterone and transformed into males—which, because they retain the genetic makeup of females, sire females only.

Diploid salmon of grotesque and unnatural proportions are being contrived by dosing the fry with bioengineered chicken and cow growth hormones. Next step, now in progress: Equip salmon with the genes to make the hormones themselves.

A natural antifreeze has been isolated in winter flounder and is about to be transferred to stripers and trout. Supposedly this will enable them to reside in colder habitats where they will have who knows what impact.

Finally, America is addressing the Divine error of fish bones. One of the grandest things about fried or broiled trout is the way one can fillet them with a fork, peeling away the sweet, firm meat and leaving a perfect, bare skeleton of the sort trafficked in by cartoon cats. There is, in this simple act, something eminently natural and satisfying, such as popping meat from a lobster tail. Even those who have never eaten whole fish can, if possessed of fingers and functional intelligence, be taught in seconds to debone a cooked trout. When people say they do not like trout bones, it means they have mutilated the trout they have eaten.

To deal with such incompetence, the Clear Springs Trout Company in Buhl, Idaho, is producing a fish to match—the boneless trout. Already culturists have done away with the pin bones in the abdomen. Inevitably, the boneless trout—the ultimate symbol of our current taste in "natural" objects—will find its way into state stocking programs. What, I wonder, will Bob Smith say when he hauls one of these amorphous blobs of protoplasm onto the bank and it collapses like a jellyfish?

Conservation

IT IS AN AXIOM among outdoors people that "things aren't as good as they used to be." Things being fishing and hunting (or backpacking, surfing, birding, skiing mountaineering and so on), and the reasons for their decline being the pressure of development, pollution and the wants of every special interest imaginable—including the anglers, shooters, and skiers themselves, as their numbers increase. The common wisdom is that they aren't making any more trout streams. Or elk ranges or waterfowl flyways. And we're loving the ones we have to death.

But is this really the case? It happens that we *are* making more trout streams. Or at least fixing the old ones. Hydrologists and aquatic biologists across North America are hanging out their shingles as stream doctors, for hire to landowners or fishing clubs to restore waterways to trout and salmon caliber. This can be as simple as fencing off cattle that have been flattening the banks and eating the streamside vegetation, or may involve concerted political action to curb the spill from a paper mill.

In 1982 I visited Lee and Joan Wulff's fly-fishing school, in New York's Catskill Mountains, for the first time. Lee was then 77 and had been a leading light of American sportfishing for 50 years. He is the man who said, back in the 1930s, "a good gamefish is too valuable to be caught only once," and then set about spearheading the catch-and-release movement. At that school session Lee said something else that made an impression. He said, "About eight or ten years ago, trout fishing in this country turned the corner. Trout fishing is, overall, better now than it was." I asked him about it later, and he confirmed that belief.

Thanks to catch-and-release, slot limits, no-kill, tough dam-licensing procedures (and permit reviews for old dams), growing environmental awareness and legislation, the burgeoning popularity of fly-fishing and its sporting ethics, and a host of other factors, the short-term prospects for trout and salmon (and many other gamefish) do seem promising, at least in North America. Yet today, while we appear to have headed off many local and regional threats, progress is threatened by environmental damage of truly global proportions. The atmosphere itself, which binds together every aspect of life on earth, is being poisoned by industrial waste—and now, when we need them the most, the great forests that have freshened and filtered the air for eons are being leveled.

It seems we must break things before we fix them. If but 10 percent of the attention paid to restoring the whooping crane or the panda today had been applied to those species 30 years earlier, they would never have gotten into trouble. But that's not news. The news is that we did not let trout and salmon go to the very edge before rallying 'round. (But things had sunk pretty low before the turnaround.) The anglers who wanted to have fish to catch saved them. Once again reinforcing the axiom that a species—or a river, or a forest, or a flyway—that is unknown is in trouble because it has no guardians.

As the introduction points out, gamefish, especially the salmonids, are accurate environmental barometers. There are reasons for caring about trout and salmon that go beyond the simple appreciation of beauty or fighting spirit. Devoted anglers pride themselves on learning to understand the whole environment of their quarry. They have to, to be successful; they try to catch trout by fitting into their world and luring them with imitations of their natural food. (It's not so simple with salmon, who have come into fresh water to spawn, not to eat, yet understanding the fish's life-cycle is still the key to angling success.) Studying the fish teaches us that there are a hundred things that may throw a trout off its feed or kill it; it is a fragile organism. Anglers know there is no better indicator of the overall ecological health of a stream and its surroundings than a resident population of naturally reproducing trout, or a strong and unimpeded run of spawning salmon.

As go the wild fish, so do we. Fishermen have been the champions of trout and salmon, and the species are now accepted by informed voters everywhere as important to the quality of our lives. Today some fisheries are healthier than others, but all are under intense or growing scrutiny. And even the arguments raging over Alaskan oil spills or Norwegian hydro dams or Native American subsistence netting are wonderful signs. We don't concern ourselves with the health of a corpse.

Sportfishermen will continue to set the example in North America and the rest of the world. If something as "frivolous" as fishing for trout and salmon can prosper—or if there are simply enough people who want it to prosper—we are in better shape than we might think. But as local and regional attitudes change to reflect this, we must raise our awareness to a higher level. To lose the entire planet to global warming or acid precipitation just as its individual streams have been cleaned up would be a supreme irony.

Acknowledgements

THE AUTHOR AND PUBLISHER wish to thank Lee and Joan Wulff, Mel Krieger, John Betts, Mike and Suzie Fitzgerald, Michael McLelland, Ted Williams, and Allen and Sally Fernald. Others contributed materially to this book as well, including Bill Davies, Toshi Shimoda, John Merwin, Darrel Martin, Ron and Maggie McMillan, Tony Pawson, Nick Lyons and, of course, the 28 photographers whose skills, experience, and world travels are reflected in these images.

Portions of this book first appeared in *Fly Rod & Reel* Magazine (of which the author is the editor) and in *Gamefish of North America*, also by the author. In addition, "Frankenstein's Trout," by Ted Williams, was also published in *Audubon* Magazine. It is included here because unless its message is heeded, wild trout may be bred out of existence as governments seek to create a salmonid that can tolerate pollution—instead of cleaning up our waters so that wild fish may thrive.

Index